Getting Started on the Internet

A practical step-by-step guide for beginners

Internet Handbooks

Other titles in preparation

Getting Started
on the Internet

A practical step-by-step guide for beginners

Kye Valongo

www.**internet-handbooks**.co.uk

Other Internet Handbooks by the same author

Discussion Forums on the Internet
Internet Explorer on the Internet
Using Email on the Internet
Using Netscape on the Internet
Where to Find It on the Internet

First published in 2000 by Internet Handbooks, a Division of International Briefings Ltd, Plymbridge House, Estover Road, Plymouth PL6 7PY, United Kingdom.

Customer services tel:	(01752) 202301
Orders fax:	(01752) 202333
Customer services email:	cservs@plymbridge.com
Distributors web site:	www.plymbridge.com
Internet Handbooks web site:	www.internet-handbooks.co.uk

Note: The contents of this book are offered for the purposes of general guidance only and no liability can be accepted for any loss or expense incurred as a result of relying in particular circumstances on statements made in this book. Readers are advised to check the current position with the appropriate authorities before entering into personal arrangements.

Case studies in this book are entirely fictional and any resemblance to real persons or organisations is entirely coincidental.

Printed and bound by The Cromwell Press Ltd, Trowbridge, Wiltshire.

Contents

Contents ....

List of illustrations

Preface

. . . .

The internet grew from the desire to link computers together so people could share information. The initial network was so successful that an even bigger dream formed: that of an interconnected network of computers around the world so that people could access information and programs from anywhere on earth. (For a comprehensive history of the internet, see: http://www.delphi.com/navnet/faq/history.html).

There is no one simple definition of the internet, no single description of what it is and what it means for our future. It would be rather like trying to define the impact of 'the printed word' and the printing press in the fifteenth century, which spelled the end of the middle ages.

Here are some things we can say about the internet:

1. It is made up of millions of computers and other equipment connected together using the world's telephone systems.

2. The internet is a vast and ever-expanding ocean of useful information of every kind imaginable a fabulous resource.

3. It is a soggy marsh containing an unbelievable amount of rubbish.

4. It's a place where you can learn about anything, talk with anyone, and indulge in almost any kind of entertainment.

5. It's a place where businesses can set up for a fraction of the cost of a more traditional enterprise requiring umpteen middlemen.

6. It is a global phenomenon, which takes less and less account of national boundaries and national institutions.

The benefits

The most amazing thing about the internet is that it allows ordinary people to bypass the middlemen – big business, national governments and media empires – who have long dominated our lives. With the internet, anyone can now see through the hogwash, half-truths and superstition fed to us by those traditionally in control of information. Throughout the world, we are at the start of a social and historical revolution.

The internet is starting to connect with every aspect of our lives television, shopping, mobile phones, entertainment, health, education, personal finance, law, news, and government. It may even be keeping an eye on the contents of your fridge. Internet connections will become faster, and access much cheaper. Soon there will be many powerful new features, such as videoconferencing and on-demand television.

There are huge benefits in all this – far wider choice and lower prices for consumers, an amazing variety of new business and work opportunities, and access to a vast amount of information and services covering every topic imaginable. The internet can be a huge support, for example whether you are a student at school or college, a professional person or business manager, saving or borrowing money, or in need of specialist medical information.

The dark side

But there is a darker side to this global revolution. The internet can appear very complicated and unfathomable many ordinary people. A huge social and economic divide is likely to develop between firms and individuals who embrace the internet and those who do not. Individuals without internet savvy will find themselves disadvantaged in many ways in education, in the workplace, and in ordinary life.

The unprecedented freedom of the internet is seen by most governments and vested interests as a huge threat: ordinary people everywhere are demanding much fuller information about government, public bodies, big business, and science. They are increasingly questioning the domination and ethics of those in control.

There lies the great truth about the internet: you are in control. The internet is a vast ocean of information and services. You can either drown in it or use it to travel anywhere on earth. To be able to use it, you have to be willing to toughen up and use the many tools available. You have to fight through the rubbish and get to the real information. You must learn to defend yourself against the many new threats you will encounter.

It's very much a DIY world in which it pays to become information-smart. You need to understand when a web site, or a piece of software, or an internet service provider, is giving you biased information, trying to extract personal information from you, or damage your interests or your computer in some way. You must learn to distinguish quality information and quality links from con-artists and time-wasters.

The journey is exciting and enormously worthwhile, if sometimes a little scary, but for good or ill it represents our future.

Good luck with your journey!

Kye Valongo

kyevalongo@internet-handbooks.co.uk

1 Getting connected

In this chapter we will explore:

▶ *a computer and some bits*
▶ *linking up to a telephone line or mobile phone*
▶ *getting an internet service provider*
▶ *signing up and installing the internet software*
▶ *a word about passwords*

. . . .

A computer and some bits

To connect to the net, you need a computer with a modem attached. (Later, we'll also show how you can connect using a specially equipped mobile phone or television.)

The advice in this chapter is primarily intended for people with personal computers. You will probably be using a Microsoft Windows operating system, such as Windows95, Windows98 or Windows2000. Windows has become a *de facto* world standard. Different advice may be required if you use an Apple Macintosh computer, which uses a different operating system.

What is a modem?
In essence, a modem is a device that enables your computer to access your telephone line. As such, the modem is the key piece of equipment for linking up to the internet. The better the modem, the smoother will be your internet experience. Cheaper modems can cause problems with Windows. Often they are slower and less reliable. A good modem will soon pay for itself by cutting down on your telephone bill.

Buying a modem
Most computers today are fitted with an internal modem. Later on, you may want to buy a better modem to keep pace with new technology.

Fig. 1. Internal and external modems (left and right). Internal ones are cheaper, but more complicated to install. The external ones are easy to plug in and use, and offer portability.

Getting connected..

Here are some tips on buying a modem:

1. Get the fastest modem you can afford. They typically cost £50 to £100.

2. Buy one of the better-known brands, Hayes or Rockwell for example. This should ensure reliability and compatibility with your computer software.

3. Internal modems are cheaper and tidier (out of sight and out of mind), but they can be complicated to install.

4. External modems are much easier to install, and it's easy to move them to another computer if you need to.

Installing a new modem
The physical procedure for installing a new modem varies and, especially with internal modems, it can be particularly tricky. You'll need to get inside your computer. If you are at all unsure, get the help of someone who knows what to do. That does not mean your friend's son who is 'a computer genius', but someone who will be covered by insurance should a problem occur. Your local computer shop, for example, will probably have installed hundreds of modems or will be able to point you in the direction of someone who has.

If you feel confident enough to install a modem yourself, follow the printed instructions and diagram included with the package. If there are no instructions, go and swap it for a decent brand.

An external modem is about the size of a small paperback book. It's basically a question of plugging one cable into the back of the computer, and the other into a telephone socket. You then pop a disk into the computer to load the software which runs the modem.

Detecting the modem
Windows should detect your modem when you first switch it on after installing it. Check that it has done so, and run through the steps. Otherwise, start the Modem Installation Wizard like this:

1. Open your Start menu (figure 2).

2. Select Settings, then Control Panel (figure 2).

3. Double-click the Modems icon to get to the Modem Properties window (figure 3).

4. Click Add, and follow the instructions (figure 4)

Still have problems? It shouldn't be your fault. Go back to the person who installed your modem, complain, then tell them you want it set up correctly.

Linking up to a telephone line or mobile phone

The next step after installing your modem is to check you have a working

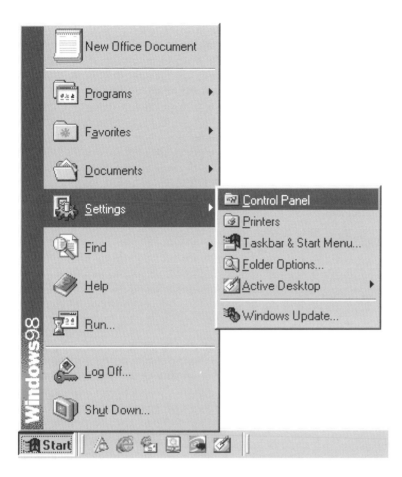

Fig. 2. Looking for the Control Panel on a personal computer. Click Start, Settings, then Control Panel.

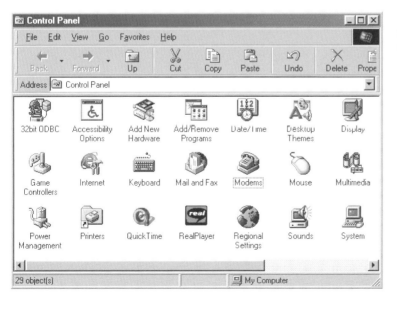

Fig. 3. Looking for the modem on a personal computer. In Control Panel, click the icon labelled Modems.

Getting connected..

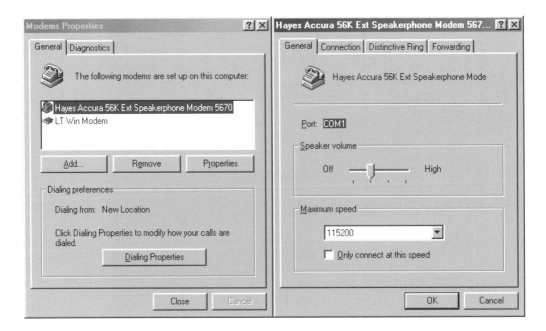

Fig. 4. Modem properties are shown on the left. This computer has two modems. Clicking Properties will display the details of the highlighted modem (in this case a Hayes Accura modem).

telephone connection. Any normal household telephone line will do for the vast majority of internet users. Make sure the thin modem cable attached to the back of the computer (or attached to the external modem) is plugged into the telephone socket on the wall.

If a fast internet connection is specially important to you for some reason, you could consider using BT's Home Highway service. Occasionally, you may want to send large files or images by email. If this is only once in a blue moon, then you can afford to wait an hour or so to take advantage of the off-peak telephone rate for evenings and weekends. However, if you need to send large numbers of files as part of your business (or can afford it anyway), then consider BT's Home Highway Service.

BT's Home Highway Service
http://www.homehighway.bt.com/
Home Highway will speed things up considerably. It can become expensive, but if you use the internet heavily, then it will save you time and possibly money. For information dial the operator on 150, or visit the web site above.

Mobile phones and PDAs
It's estimated that two billion people will be using mobile phones by 2003. Many of them will want to access the internet. Obviously, the kind of information shown on a two-inch mobile phone screen will be limited, but for certain purposes like buying a book or checking a timetable, the mobile phone is ideal. You can also send email, book cinema tickets, find a recipe, or even play a computer game.

It's common for web sites to display hundreds of links on a single

14

Fig. 5. The web site of BT HomeHighway. Although somewhat more expensive than an ordinary phone line, the service offers more flexibility and faster access to the internet.

page. This obviously isn't feasible on the screen of a mobile phone, or even on the larger screen of a PDA.

▶ *PDA* – Personal data assistant: any kind of hand-held computer, mobile internet phone or organiser.

Viewing many of the web sites as they are designed today – with large graphics and layouts meant to be viewed on a computer monitor – would be impossible. But developers are beginning to design sites appropriate to the much smaller screen. There is even a special search engine for mobile phones at http://www.wapwarp.com (see page 29 for an explanation of search engines). The technology behind this is called WAP.

▶ *WAP* – Wireless applications protocol, the technology that allows web sites and applications to be created so they can be displayed and run on mobile phones and PDAs.

WAP-enabled web sites will let you choose one of up to nine links, plus a tenth option that will move you back up to the previous level of the site – one for each of the ten digits. The sites themselves need to be this simple so they make sense on the tiny screens of mobile phones.

Getting an internet service provider

The final step in getting onto the internet is to sign up with an ISP, or internet service provider. An ISP is a company that connects your computer to the internet. It enables you to dial up to the internet using a special local or national rate telephone number. A current trend is for ISPs to provide users with unlimited access to a freephone number in return for paying a fixed monthly charge. The charge remains fixed regardless of how long you spend connected 'online' – or when.

With all ISPs, you only pay for the (usually local) call to your ISP. Even though you may be viewing information on a computer in Hong Kong or Australia, there are no international phone bills to worry about.

Choosing an ISP
There are four main types of ISP:

1. ones that charge nothing at all
2. ones that charge for supplying extra services not available on the internet
3. ones that charge a monthly fee in return for better service and support
4. ones that offer a freephone connection.

In practice, the first is the most sensible choice. There are lots of reliable free ISPs out there. Once you are connected to the vast internet, you will be able to find all the services and content you will ever need without having to pay extra for the 'exclusive' services that some ISPs offer.

Freephone ISPs are becoming much more popular. Of course, there is usually a catch. Most of the 0800 number ISPs require you to fill in a questionnaire with personal details, and they then sell this information to other companies. They may also bombard you, and anyone you email, with advertising.

Two freephone ISPs are:

▶ CallNet – call 0800 058 0800 or visit http://www.callnet.co.uk

▶ Strayduck – call 0845 660 9000 or visit http://www.strayduck.com

There are hundreds of ISPs to choose from. The most popular ones in Britain include Freeserve, America OnLine, Demon Net, Virgin Net, BTinternet, Compuserve and Globalnet. Many of them are free apart from the telephone costs. If you 'sign up' with a free ISP, there is nothing preventing you from dropping that one whenever you want and moving to another. In fact you can sign up to several at once, and switch between them.

To find the latest information on free ISPs, buy an illustrated monthly internet magazine such *as Practical Internet*. Alternatively, once you have a connection, take a look at Net for Nowt at http://www.n4n.co.uk for a list of the latest free ISPs.

Probably the best known free ISP in Britain is Freeserve. If you want to sign up with them, pick up a CD from Dixons, Curry's, PC World or The Link. Another, smaller and probably faster, ISP is Madasafish. To get hold of their free CD you can send an email to:

molly@madasafish.com

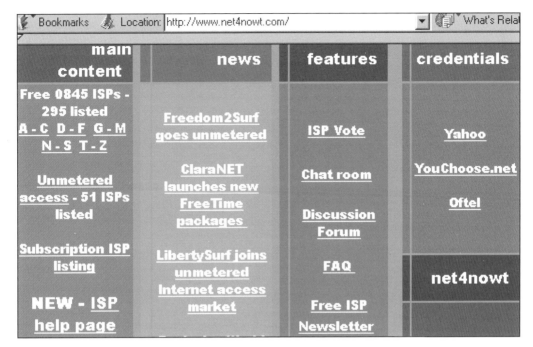

main content

Free 0845 ISPs - 295 listed
A - C   D - F   G - M
N - S   T - Z

Unmetered access - 51 ISPs listed

Subscription ISP listing

NEW - ISP help page

news

Freedom2Surf goes unmetered

ClaraNET launches new FreeTime packages

LibertySurf joins unmetered Internet access market

features

ISP Vote

Chat room

Discussion Forum

FAQ

Free ISP Newsletter

credentials

Yahoo

YouChoose.net

Oftel

net4nowt

Signing up and installing the internet software

Signing up is simple. Just pop the CD into your computer, sit back, and let it run. The installation program will automatically take you through various steps. It will ask you questions along the way, such as your name, address and other information. It will also ask you to choose a user name and a password.

Most CDs include all the internet software and Help files you will need. These typically include a web browser like Internet Explorer or Netscape Navigator (so you can view web pages), an email client like Outlook Express or Netscape Messenger (so you can send and receive emails), and assorted other useful programs. If all goes smoothly, you will be able to send and receive email without having to go through any complicated setting up.

If the CD installation fails for some reason, you can set up your internet connection manually on a Windows PC. You will just need to know your ISP's dial-up telephone number, your username, and your password:

Setting up an internet connection manually
1. Click on the icon on your desktop called My Computer.
2. Open the folder called Dial-Up Networking.
3. Click the icon called Make New Connection.
4. In the New Connection Wizard type in the name of your ISP.
5. Click Next.
6. Type in the dial-up phone number of your ISP.
7. Click Next.
8. Click Finish.

Fig. 6. Net4Nowt offers a guide to UK internet service providers (ISPs). Did you know that under a new UK law, British ISPs must give the police total access to your emails and lists of the web sites you have viewed (Regulation of Investigatory Powers Act).

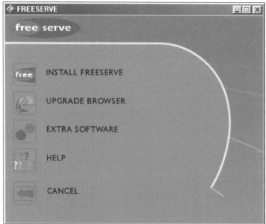

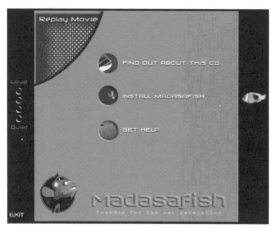
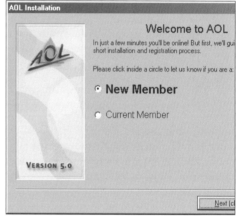

Fig. 7. Sample ISP installation software. Most ISPs supply customers with an easy-to-use CD-ROM. Pop it into your computer, and it will install everything you need to connect to and use the internet. Illustrated are Freeserve, Virgin Net, Madasafish and America OnLine.

You should now notice a new icon in your dial-up networking folder. To connect to the internet, double-click this new icon. Type in your password, click on Connect, and your computer will dial up your ISP. You will hear it dialling. Hopefully, within a few seconds you will be connected to the internet. To make it easier to connect each time in future, you could create a little shortcut on your desktop:

(a) Right-click the new icon in your Dial-Up Networking folder.

(b) Select Create Shortcut.

(c) You will be asked if you want the icon on your desktop.

(d) Click Yes. And there it is!

A word about passwords

A password can be compared to the key of a padlock – just as some locks are easy to open with a bent piece of wire, some passwords are easy to guess.

A weak password is like a key left under the doormat – an invitation to

Fig. 8. Dialing up the internet on a personal computer. Click My Computer, then Dial-Up Networking. The right-hand screen shows the internet service provider(s) installed on your computer (here, Virgin Net, Freeserve, and Madasafish). Click one of the icons to access the internet.

Fig. 9. From Dial-Up Networking (figure 8) you can make a new connection with an internet service provider.

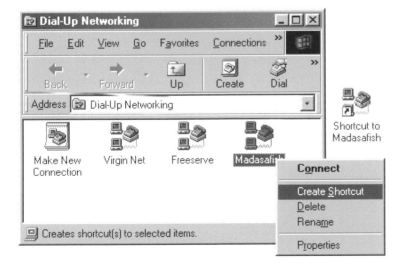

Fig. 10. Creating a handy short cut on your desktop will make it quick and easy for you to access the internet. Highlight the icon (here, Madasafish), right-click your mouse, and click Create Shortcut. The shortcut will instantly appear on your desktop, as illustrated.

19

anyone. Hackers, mischief-makers and work colleagues can all take advantage of a weak password.

Don't make the mistake of thinking that you have nothing to hide; there is often more at stake than having someone read your email or change your web site. Once someone has discovered your password, they will have access to an alternative identity, yours. To all outside appearances, they are you. If they send an insulting email message; if they try to break into a bank's computer system; if they want to swap child pornography with others, they can do it all in your name. It is going to take some fast talking to explain to the police why, for example, a person using your internet account has just replaced the Queen's portrait with a picture of a half-dressed supermodel, or worse.

Password-cracking software is freely available over the internet and elsewhere. It tries thousands of passwords tirelessly and relentlessly until it gains entry. Once a program such as this is set to work, it can sometimes detect a weak password in literally less than a second. It is estimated that 20% of passwords can be worked out in as short a time as this.

To make a secure password, create one with at least eight letters. It should contain a mix of upper case and lower case letters and numbers.

Some of the most common, and therefore weakest, passwords are:

password	sex
god	love
genius	Your name or a variation of it
Your login name	qwertyuiop (top row of the keyboard)
hacker	

Do any of these sound familiar? If you use any of these, change it.

Where can I find a password that I can remember, but that others can't work out?
An easy method is to take a phrase of eight or more words. Then use the first letter of each word: 'a bird in the hand is worth two in the bush' would become:

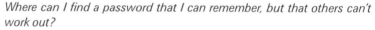

abithiwtitb

An easy way to add digits to your password is to substitute all the occurrences of the letter 'i' for 'ones' as in:

ab1th1wt1tb

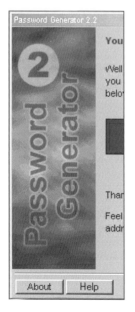

Mixing upper and lower case letters will make your password extremely hard to crack so try adding two or three. How about making every 't' uppercase, like this:

ab1Th1wT1tb

Using methods like this, you can make passwords that are easy to remember but difficult to detect. Try different combinations but please don't use this particular password. To make it even harder to crack your password, you can use computer-generated 'random' passwords. On the web, you can find sites that create random passwords. For example, look at Password Creator at:

http://www.infokeep.net/pc/

Connecting and disconnecting

Whenever any internet program needs to connect to the internet, it must first dial the number of your ISP. This is usually done automatically by the internet software on your computer (usually Internet Explorer, Outlook Express, or Netscape).

When your software tries to connect to the internet, it will start Windows Dial-Up Networking (Windows DUN). See the 'Connect To' window shown in figure 11. If for some reason, your internet program does not start DUN, you will have to connect manually:

1. Open My Computer, then the Dial-Up Networking window.

2. Click the connection for your ISP.

3. Enter your name and password.

4. Click Connect.

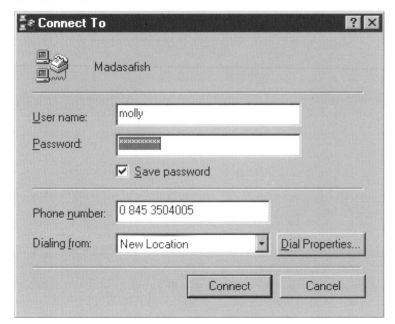

Fig. 11. A standard panel like this appears when you start connecting to the internet. To connect, you must enter your username and password. Then click Connect. Some ISPs also require you to enable CLID (caller line identification). If so, put 1470 before the ISP's phone number.

The 'Connecting to' window should now appear as your computer dials into the ISP's number. If this fails, you may not have DUN installed, or may have to re-install it. To make sure you have Dial-Up Networking installed:

1. On your desktop, double-click the icon My Computer. Then, if you do not see an icon for Dial-Up Networking:

Getting connected...

2. Open the Start menu, select Settings, then Add/Remove Programs.

3. Click Communications, and then Details.

4. Select the Dial-Up Networking check box, and click OK.

Fig. 12. Connected! To show that you are online, a little icon will appear in the bottom right of your screen. It resembles two tiny computer screens. You can double-click on it to display the DUN window (figure 11). Right-click on it when you wish to disconnect from the internet.

Once you are connected, the 'Connecting to' notice disappears and DUN minimises to a small icon on your Start menu. If you double-click this icon it will reappear as in figure 13. To disconnect, simply click the 'Disconnect' button. You can also right-click on the small icon on your Windows toolbar. To prevent DUN dialling or to interrupt it before it finishes, just click the 'Cancel' button.

Dial-up Networking icon minimised

Fig. 13. Connected to Madasafish. The DUN window tells you how long you have been connected to the internet. It also gives you an indication of how fast your connection is. You can also click here when you wish to disconnect from the internet.

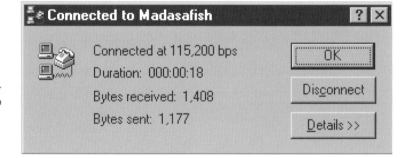

Other Internet Handbooks to help you

Using Email on the Internet
Internet Explorer on the Internet
Using Netscape on the Internet

Visit the free Internet HelpZone at
www.internet-handbooks.co.uk
Helping you master the internet

22

2 Exploring the world wide web

In this chapter we will explore:

▶ *a window to the world – browsing the web*
▶ *visiting your first site*
▶ *offline viewing*
▶ *your tour guides: internet directories and search engines*
▶ *directories*
▶ *search engines*
▶ *doing keyword searches*
▶ *metasearch tools*
▶ *remembering your favourite visits*
▶ *total immersion: the active desktop*
▶ *sites and sounds: multimedia*

. . . .

From the home user's point of view, the web is made up of documents called web pages. These web pages are rather like the text and pictures you see in a magazine, but the components could be located anywhere in the world and you might never know it. Occasionally, you will come across web pages that have more advanced content such as animated images, sound clips or even short video clips.

You could be looking at a page that is located on a computer in Spain that has been created by someone living in Manchester, and the pictures on the page are located on a computer in India. You would not be aware of the international nature of the page just by looking at it, because internet technology recognises no national boundaries. What's more, you can add to this information world by creating your own web site. The variety on the web is practically endless. You will find something about everything – no matter how obscure or bizarre – somewhere on the web.

Usually, web pages are grouped together into web sites. A web site is a collection of web pages with a similar theme, again similar to a magazine. The BBC web site, for example, follows the theme of television and radio. It includes features such as news, entertainment, films and others that you would associate with the BBC. There are probably thousands of pages constituting the BBC web site.

A window to the world – browsing the web

When you view web pages, you are said to be browsing, or surfing, the web. Popular words such as browsing and surfing imply that you are physically moving around the web, but this is misleading and makes it hard to appreciate what is really happening. You may fidget or stand up and stretch occasionally, but that is usually as far as you can move physically without losing sight of your monitor.

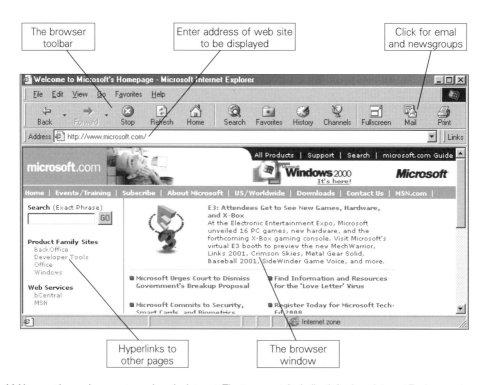

The browser toolbar

Enter address of web site to be displayed

Click for emal and newsgroups

Hyperlinks to other pages

The browser window

Fig. 14. You must have a browser to explore the internet. The two great rivals (both free) are Internet Explorer and Netscape Navigator. Of the two, Microsoft's Internet Explorer is slightly easier to use, and integrates better with other Microsoft programs.

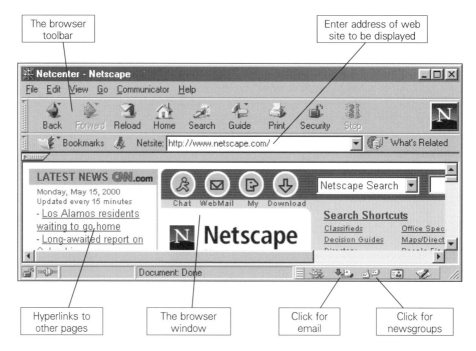

The browser toolbar

Enter address of web site to be displayed

Hyperlinks to other pages

The browser window

Click for email

Click for newsgroups

Fig. 15. What the browser Netscape Navigator looks like. Its layout and features are very similar to those of Internet Explorer (which followed Netscape into the market). Running across the top of the screen is a toolbar, full of useful controls.

▶ *Browser* – A special computer program that allows you to retrieve and view web sites. By far the best-known browsers are Microsoft's Internet Explorer, and Netscape Navigator. They are very similar. Most new computers come pre-loaded with Internet Explorer. In any case, your ISP's CD will install one or the other for you.

What actually happens when you view a web page? The page components are copied ('downloaded') from wherever in the world they are stored, and reproduced ('saved') onto your computer. Perhaps a better word for browser would be 'page fetcher' or 'internet downloader'. This downloading is almost invisible to you. All you see is a momentary message or two at the bottom of the browser and then, after a short while, the web page itself will appear. So, whenever you view a web page, you are viewing a document that has just been saved on your computer.

Visiting your first site

Viewing a web page is simplicity in itself. Try this: connect to the internet according to the instructions of your internet service provider. Then start your browser program by clicking the appropriate icon. You will now see a web page gradually appearing as it is retrieved in stages. First the text will become visible, followed by the images one by one. It typically takes twenty to sixty seconds for a web page to load into view.

Fig. 16. Changing your home page ('start up' page). This is the page that is loaded when-ever you start your browser. ISPs often set it up to be their own web site's home page, but you can easily change it to something else, such as your favourite news or entertainment site.

By default, every time a browser starts, it tries to find a page called the 'home page'. Initially, the home page is specified by the browser manufacturer or by your ISP. It is usually one of the main pages of that company, Netscape or Microsoft for example, or Freeserve or Virgin Net.

▶ *ISP* – Internet service provider, the company that enables you to access the internet. It usually also provides you with the necessary internet software and other online services such as news, weather reports, and chat rooms.

After the home page has loaded into view, you will want to explore a different site. This too is a simple step. All but the most basic web pages contain references or links ('hyperlinks') to pages on the same site and on other sites. These links contain information that tells your browser where the page is located. You click on any link with your mouse cursor, and the page at that location is displayed on your screen.

Links are easy to spot. You can recognise them in a number of ways.

Exploring the world wide web ....

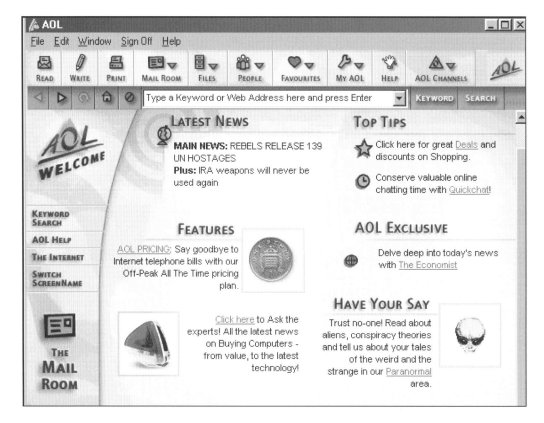

Fig. 17. America Online has its own special browser, illustrated here. Like Internet Explorer and Netscape, it has a toolbar across the top, a box near the top to enter web site addresses, and a main browser window in the middle where web pages are displayed.

Underlined text usually means that it is a link. Often these links are arranged in a menu system at one edge of a web page.

(a) A text link might look like this: Click here for more info.

(b) Other links have the appearance of little coloured buttons or arrows.

(c) If your mouse cursor changes from an arrow into a pointing hand, it means it is on a link.

Whenever you click on a link, you are telling your browser to find and retrieve the document at the 'location' that the link refers to. The page you are then looking at will then disappear to be replaced by the new page retrieved.

Fig. 18. Hyperlinks. Whenever your mouse cursor changes into a pointing hand, you know that it is positioned on a hyperlink. Clicking on the link takes you to another page on that site or another web site elsewhere.

Finding a web page is very like finding someone's house. First of all you need to know the address. The address of a web page is called the URL (uniform resource locator). It is unique, just like a house address. You use the URL of a page to 'point' your browser at that page.

▶ *URL* – Uniform resource locator, the unique address of a web page, image or other document on the internet. An example of a URL is:

http://ukdirectory.com

It looks complicated and makes little sense to the eye. But if you study it, you will be able to make out the words 'directory' and 'UK'. You might then guess that it is the URL of a directory of web sites in the UK. Your guess would be right.

Not all URLs are so meaningful. All you really need to know is that your browser will take you to the right site if you type in its address correctly. In that respect, your browser is just like a taxi – you don't need to know where the address is, or even which language it is in, as long as your taxi driver (browser) does.

Offline viewing

Since web pages are retrieved and stored on your computer, it should follow that you will still be able to view them after you disconnect. And so you can to some extent. The browser keeps some of the pages on your computer's hard disk in a place called the cache. The pages are kept in the cache until it becomes full. Then, the older pages are automatically deleted to make room for new ones.

Try it yourself with a site called Pure Fiction. It's 'for anybody who loves to read, or aspires to write, best-selling fiction'. Go online and type the following URL into your browser, and press 'enter':

http://www.purefiction.com

Wait until the page finishes loading. Then press the key shortcut 'Control-D' to add the page to your favourites menu in Internet Explorer. (Netscape Navigator uses the same key shortcut but calls the stored URLs 'bookmarks'.) Now disconnect.

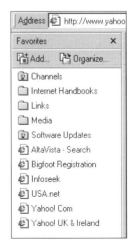

▶ *Key shortcut* – Two keys pressed at the same time. Usually they are the 'control' key (Ctrl), 'Alt' key, or 'Shift' key, combined with a letter or number. For example, to use 'Control-D', press 'Control', tap the 'D' key once firmly, then take your finger off the 'Control' key.

To prove offline viewing works, first of all make sure you are offline. Then start your browser program but don't let it connect to the internet. Now do the following steps:

1. Select the File menu, then Work Offline (Navigator: Go Offline).

2. Open the Favourites Menu (Bookmarks).

3. Select the Pure Fiction entry.

4. Watch the site load. Simple.

You do not have to disconnect each time you add a page to your favourites. Just press Control-D and move on. Offline viewing is especially useful if you want to read a page with lots of text such as an in-depth news report or a short story. Of course, many sites such as news sources change daily or more often. To retrieve the latest news you would need to connect again to refresh the site's content.

Your tour guides: internet directories and search engines

Trying to find anything on the internet without help can be like trying to find a needle in a haystack. Luckily, abundant help is available on the web in the form of sites like directories and search engines. These powerful sites are designed and maintained to help you to find the information you want. Using these tools efficiently is one of the keys to finding and keeping up to date with good sites.

▶ *Directory* – A special web site which consists of information about other sites. The information is classified by subject area and further subdivided into smaller categories.

▶ *Search engine* – A directory compiled with the help of a special computer program. The program automatically scans the world wide web, storing and categorising information about sites as it goes.

Directories

Online directories are very similar to the familiar Yellow Pages. Sites are classified by subject area and further subdivided into smaller categories. Unlike with Yellow Pages, you can enter a keyword and let the site do the searching for you.

- Higher Education *(13204)* N
- Instructional Technology *(*
- Journals *(27)*
- Literacy *(9)*
- News and Media *(95)* NEW!
- Organisations *(2970)* NEW!
- Policy *(47)* NEW!
- Programmes *(290)* NEW!
- Reform *(50)* NEW!
- Schools *(46281)* NEW!
- Special Education *(173)* NEW
- Standards and Testing *(69)*
- Statistics *(7)*
- Teaching *(102)*
- Theory and Methods *(618)*
- Web Directories *(50)*

Yahoo!
http://uk.yahoo.com
One of the best known directories is Yahoo!. It contains information on hundreds of thousands of sites from the home pages of private individuals to the web sites of the largest corporations. Yahoo! organises everything by categories, like a library organises its books. There are sections for entertainment, arts and humanity, business and economy, computer and the internet, and so on. The classifications start general and become more specific as you make choices. For instance, if you choose 'Entertainment', you are shown a page where the selections are broken down further into such topics as 'Food and drink', 'Games', and 'Music'. By following the links, you will eventually come to the topic area you are interested in; you will see a list of relevant web URLs and a short description for each site, for example a list of vegetarian restaurants in London.

It is very much like climbing a tree: first you clamber up the main trunk, then onto one of the main branches, and then to smaller branches until you find the information you want – the fruit. The sites listed in a directory are placed there by humans. If nobody 'registers' the URL and a description of a site with a directory, you will not find it. In that case you would probably do better with a search engine.

Fig.19. Internet searches. The Yahoo! directory is one of the best known and probably the most visited directory on the internet. It has a separate site for the UK and many for other countries around the world.

Search engines

Search engines have information about many more sites. A search engine automatically scans the web following links from site to site storing and categorising information as it goes. As it stops at each site, it finds keywords to add to its index. Search engines also keep their information current by constantly searching for new sites and updating the ones already in their lists. Some search engines collect specific information limited to a subject area (such as education) or a particular country (such as Brazil or the UK).

Imagine a little robot wandering around the web from site to site, busily collecting information like a bee collecting pollen. This gives some idea of what is happening. These automatic systems have been termed robots, spiders and web crawlers – cute if you are not afraid of creepy-crawlies.

The large number of sites listed on search engines makes them more difficult to use. However, once mastered, search engines can be much more effective than directories. To use them to their full, you need to know how to use keywords.

Exploring the world wide web ....

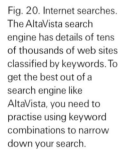

Yahoo! search, please use
ect a search method:
- ⊙ Intelligent default
- ○ An exact phrase matc
- ○ Matches on all words
- ○ Matches on any word

Doing keyword searches

With search engines and directories, you can search for sites matching keywords that you type into a form on the search site. Keywords help you to:

1. find sites on a specific subject
2. filter out the unwanted information

Using the wrong combination of keywords can bring you hundreds of thousands of matches or none at all. It is like opening a child's toy cupboard – you never know what is going to fall out until you open it. Using keywords effectively may seem complicated at first, but using the right syntax and combination of keywords will give you a manageable and useful list. One that is relevant to your area of interest but not too short a list that there is little to choose from.

Let's take an example. Suppose you want to find some sites that deal with house auctions. Let's first go to a search engine called AltaVista at:

Fig. 20. Internet searches. The AltaVista search engine has details of tens of thousands of web sites classified by keywords. To get the best out of a search engine like AltaVista, you need to practise using keyword combinations to narrow down your search.

http://www.altavista.com

1. Type *buying a house* in the search box.
2. Click the Search button.

My attempt came back with thousands of matches – not many of them were relevant to auctions and some of them were about buying something else. The search engines were looking separately for the words 'buying' or 'house' so there were topics such as 'buying a new car' and

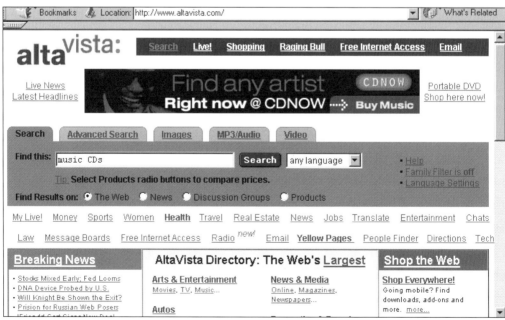

'decorating your house', and many others weird and wonderful sites. Adding more keywords made it even worse. Entering *buying a house in an auction* returned over 20,000 matches it would take weeks to check them all.

Enclosing a phrase in quotes usually narrows down a search by ensuring that only references using the whole phrase will be listed, excluding all those ufologists and masseurs. Using:

''house auctions''

returned 5,000 matches – better, but it would mean hours of work to find the best sites. The next step is to exclude the US sites part we are only interested in buying a house in the UK.

''house auctions NOT USA''

came up with no matches because the phrase inside the quotes is meaningless – remember the search engine looks for the exact phrase if it is enclosed in quotes. However we can split it into two phrases. Adding the special word 'NOT' commands the search engine to ignore sources containing 'USA' anywhere in the text.

''house auctions'' NOT USA

brought up about 1,000 matches. Not too bad, but the list contained lots of entries for one particular company that dealt only with commercial property Wright and Sons. To get rid of those entries the keyword phrase was changed to:

''house auctions'' NOT USA NOT commercial

Now there was a list of about 35 – ideal.

Another special keyword is OR. This word is useful if two or more different names or terms refer to the subject you want. It is also useful if you are interested in either of two or more options. Suppose your child wants to find sites about either dragons or witches. You could enter:

dragons OR witches

A third useful word is AND. This forces the search site to look for both words in the search. Say your child is interested in knights slaying dragons but is scared of trolls. Entering

knights AND dragons NOT trolls

would ensure that the sites with trolls would be excluded. These features can be combined to give you very precise control over a search, as in:

''short stories'' AND witches NOT trolls

(Note: search engines can be fussy about which type of quotes are used)

Exploring the world wide web ....

This phrase picks out short stories about witches, but not if they contain trolls.

Some search engines treat capitalised words as different from those in just lowercase letters. If you don't capitalise a word, the engine will search for both capitals and lower case. If you add a single capital letter in the word, the engine will search for that exact capitalisation and no other.

Searching is often a matter of juggling with keywords until you have found a number of matches you feel able to handle. Too many and you should try to make the search more specific. Too few and you should either use more general terms or find an alternative keyword. For example, instead of house try property.

Search engines differ in the syntax of search phrases. Some may use single quotes but others only double. Some may not recognise the special words such as AND, OR, NOT etc. To get the most out of a search engine, it is helpful to know the syntax it uses. Aim to stick to a few favourite search sites and, once you become familiar with their quirks, you will be able to find anything you want.

These techniques should be sufficient for most searches, but for more information about keywords go to one or both of these sites:

The Spider's Apprentice
http://www.monash.com/spidap.html
http://daphne.palomar.edu/TGSEARCH/

Advantages of directories	Disadvantages of directories
Directories are easier to browse at leisure, something you can't do very well with a keyword search engine.	You may have to branch through the categories repeatedly before arriving at the right page.
Reports from a search engine are not evaluated but, in a directory, human beings have evaluated each page listed. Sites are only listed if they are of acceptable quality.	If you're looking for some obscure topic, the people that maintain the directory may have excluded those pages. Search engines would be a better strategy.
	Directories are often several months behind the times because of the need for human organisation.
Advantages of search engines	Disadvantages of search engines
If you've used the right keyword strategy, you can quickly find the relevant web pages.	Keyword searching can be difficult to get right.
You can find pages that human experts (of the directories) would exclude from their lists.	It may be difficult or impossible to use a keyword search if the vocabulary of the subject is unfamiliar.
New web sites are accessible within days or even hours after publication.	You must have a clearer idea of what you're looking for.
	Search engines don't evaluate the pages they find and a certain amount of poor quality pages will be displayed.
	No single engine searches the entire internet, so it's often necessary to search several engines.

Metasearch tools

Thousands of different search engines are available. They cover both general areas and specific subjects. Some are particularly effective and sophisticated, but none is comprehensive. Most of them only have a small database of sites, or they may not be up to date (some sites take weeks to update their database). Consequently, you may need to use several search engines before you are satisfied that you have found everything you require. A metasearch engine can save you the trouble of using many different sites to run your search, or it may point you to a search engine that you didn't know about.

A metasearch engine is simply a site that sends a keyword search to many different search engines and directories. In this way, you can harness many search engines from one place. This kind of site is especially useful if you have found no information using search engines. Sometimes, if you are trying to find out about an obscure topic or one that is very new, many search engines may not have found a site, or the site designer may not have publicised it effectively.

One of the best metasearch sites is:

The Big Hub
http://www.thebighub.com
This has thousands of databases to choose from. If you want to find something that may be rare or unusual, this is a good place to start. It is an easy site to use and provides an excellent base camp from which you can explore the web and find information. This kind of site can easily bury you under a mountain of information, so be very specific in your search keywords and phrases.

Remembering your favourite visits

Internet Explorer Favourites
When you come across a web site that you may want to revisit, you can add its address to a special list. Then, the next time you want to visit it,

Fig. 21. Adding a favourite web site to your bookmarks in Internet Explorer.

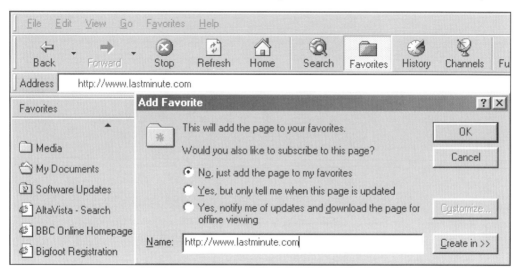

you only need to open the list and click on the entry for that site. Internet Explorer calls the list Favourites (using the US spelling 'Favorites'). To revisit a web site, just click the 'Favorites' button on the toolbar, and then click the site title in the list.

To add a web site to your favourites list:

1. Go to the web site.

2. On the Favorites menu, click Add to Favorites.

3. Type your own descriptive name for the page, if you want to.

If you have a handful of sites or pages that you visit often, you can also add them to your Links bar.

Changing the home page in your browser
If there is one particular page that you like to visit very often, you can make it your home page so that it is displayed every time you start Internet Explorer or click the 'Home' button on the toolbar.

Your home page will become your starting point on the internet. Make sure it is a page that you want to view frequently. Or make it one that you can customise to get quick access to all the information you want, such as the msn.com home page.

Fig. 22. Specifying the 'home page' which will open when your browser first starts up.

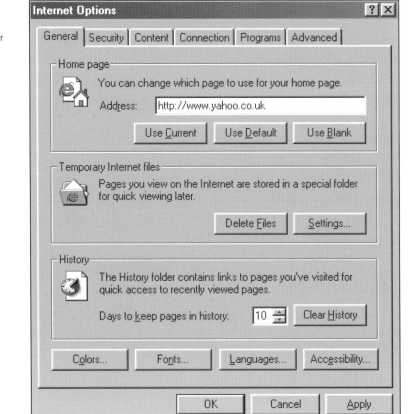

To change your home page:
Go to the page you want to appear when you start Internet Explorer.

1. Open the Tools menu and click Internet Options.

2. Click the General tab. In the Home page area, click Use Current.

3. To restore your original home page, click Use Default.

If you forget to add a web site to the Favourites list or Links bar, you can click the History button on the toolbar. The History list records the sites that you have visited recently. To go to the site, click the name of the site from the list.
   To view your history:

(a) Click the History button on your toolbar.

(b) In the History pane, click the week or day, click a web site entry to display the individual pages of that site, and then click the page title to display that page.

Netscape bookmarks
Netscape Communicator similarly lets you to save a list of favourites. Netscape calls them 'bookmarks', though. To create a bookmark:

1. Go to the web page you want to bookmark.

2. Click Bookmarks. (On Apple Macs, open the Bookmarks menu).

3. Choose Add Bookmark.

The page currently displayed will now be stored in the Bookmark menu. To revisit a web page that you have bookmarked:

(a) Click Bookmarks. (On Apple Macs, open the Bookmarks menu.)

(b) Choose the web page that you want to visit.

Total immersion: the Active Desktop

If you use Internet Explorer 4 or later, you can enhance your desktop appearance so that it behaves like a web page. You can single-click icons to open files and run programs. You can include web-like components, such as a search engine form on your desktop. You can also add components that automatically update themselves – a news ticker or a weather map, for example. You can even add components that will receive automatic updates during the day.
   To use the search form and ticker, of course, you would have to be connected to the internet, but to use the other features you would not. You can navigate your own computer almost as if it were a web site. The idea is to have a standard way of finding and using information, whether it is on your own computer or any other computer across the internet. The Active Desktop is an attempt to blur the boundary between your computer and the rest of the internet so that the two environments become almost seamless.
   The original component of the Active Desktop is the Channel Bar. You

Fig. 23. The Active Desktop. MicroSoft have taken a step towards total internet integration with their Active Desktop which makes using your computer similar to using the web.

can use the Channel Bar to quickly open Web channels from your desktop without the need to open your browser.

▶ *Channels* – Channels automatically deliver content from web sites to your computer. You can view information offline once it has been updated. When you subscribe to a channel, a component is installed onto your desktop, which is updated regularly by its provider.

Turning on the Active Desktop
If you can see the Channel bar on the desktop, the Active Desktop is already switched on. Otherwise:

1. Right-click a blank area on the desktop.
2. Open the Active Desktop item.
3. Select View as Web Page.

Fig. 24. Adding an Active Desktop component. You could install components such as weather reports, news tickers, animated clocks and cartoons, and links to your favourite web sites.

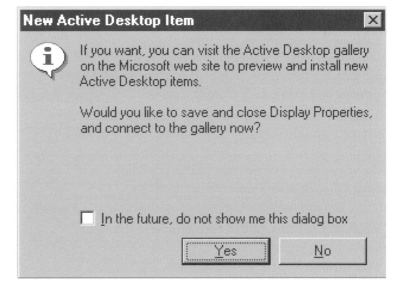

New Active Desktop Item   ☒

ⓘ If you want, you can visit the Active Desktop gallery on the Microsoft web site to preview and install new Active Desktop items.

Would you like to save and close Display Properties, and connect to the gallery now?

☐ In the future, do not show me this dialog box

Yes   No

Adding a component to your Active Desktop
There are many different components that you can use on the Active Desktop. Microsoft has its own gallery of components on its web site. To see which components are available:

1. Right-click a blank area of your desktop.
2. Select Properties, then click the Web tab.
3. Click New.
4. When you are asked if you want to go to the Active Desktop Gallery, click Yes.
5. Choose the component, if any, that interests you.

Some other components can be downloaded from sites on the internet such as the collection at http://www.iegallery.com/adc.html

Address http://www.iegallery.com/adc.html

New Components

News & Sports

Links

Miscellanious

Web Search

Newest Desktop Components

ESPN SportsZone Scorepost

DESCRIPTION: Want the latest sports scores from ESPN SportsZone™? .
AUTHOR: ESPN SportsZone

Home   Preview

Install

January 4, 1998

Desktop ScoreCenter - CBS SportsLine

DESCRIPTION: Stay up to the minute with the latest sports scores right from CBS.
AUTHOR: CBS SportsLine

Home   Preview

Install

January 4, 1998

Fortune Personal Stock Chart

DESCRIPTION: Get personalized stock information in a convenient chart format directly to your desktop with the Fortune Desktop item.
AUTHOR: Fortune

Home   Preview

Install

Removing a component from the Active Desktop

Removing one of the components on your active desktop is almost as easy:

1. Right-click your desktop.
2. Select Properties.
3. Click the Web tab.
4. Click the check box of the component to turn it off, or
5. To delete it, select the component and click the Delete button.

Fig. 25. The Internet Explorer Gallery has lots of Active Desktop components which you can download for free. These components can spruce up your desktop and keep you informed of the latest news and events while online.

Sites and sounds: multimedia

Playing multimedia files such as audio and video clips is usually easy. Most browsers come equipped with the ability to play the common multimedia files but if they encounter one that they can't, you will need to install an extra add-on or plug-in for your browser.

When you try to play a multimedia file that your browser can't handle, you may be prompted to install the add-on, or just told that the browser cannot recognise the file format. If you are prompted to install the add-on, life is easy. If not, you will have to find the relevant web site for the add-on yourself.

Stroud
http://cws.internet.com/
Many useful plug-ins and add-ons can be found at the Stroud site.

Other Internet Handbooks to help you

Where to Find It on the Internet
Exploring Yahoo! on the Internet

3 Sending and receiving email

In this chapter we will explore:

▶ *what is email?*

▶ *email addresses*

▶ *email programs*

▶ *writing and reading messages*

▶ *sending an email message*

▶ *dealing with incoming emails*

▶ *forwarding a message*

▶ *managing your messages*

Email means you can keep in touch with friends, family and business contacts who live on the other side of the world, easily and cheaply. Email has probably encouraged more people to write to one another than any other invention since the ball-point pen.

Fig. 26. Using Outlook Express. Outlook Express is the commonest and easiest email and news client to use. Most free ISP CDs set up Outlook Express for you automatically, so that you can get on with using the internet without delay.

What is email?

The internet is all about communicating with people. The most easily understood form of internet communication is probably email, short for electronic mail. Email allows you to exchange messages with anyone who has an internet connection, wherever they are in the world. Millions

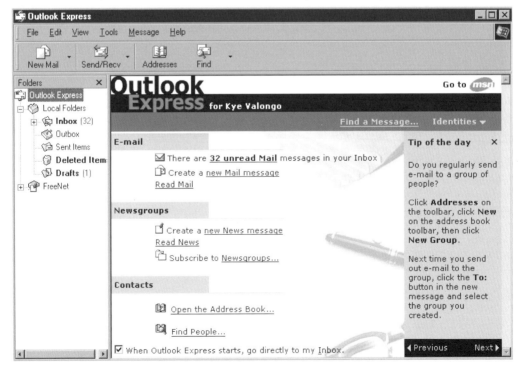

of people each day use email to send business information, private messages, and public opinions to others.

The advantage of email over telephone conversations is that the person you are communicating with doesn't have to be there at the same time as you. The message will stay around until they collect it from their ISP. Another advantage, when sending messages overseas is that the cost of sending an email message is far lower than that of an international telephone call. Email messages are also better than normal letters because they usually get there faster and don't use any paper.

What you need
To send an email message to someone, you need:

1. The person's email address.
2. An email program such as Outlook Express or Netscape Messenger. One or the other should already be installed on your computer.
3. An ISP that enables you to send and receive emails, thereby acting as your 'mail server'.

When you send an email message, your email program ('email client') contacts your ISP's email server, which then sends it over the internet to its recipient. It's rather like handing a letter to the post office. You, the client, pass the letter to the counter assistant, the server, who puts it into the postal system.

▶ *Server* – A computer program that 'serves' information to many people on a network such as the internet.

Before you can send someone an email message you need their exact address.

Email addresses

A correct email address is essential if your message is to reach the intended recipient. An example of an email address is:

admin@ukwriters.com

All email addresses look similar. Their basic form is:

username@domain.com

1. 'Username' is usually the name or nickname that you use to log onto your ISP.
2. *@* is called the 'at' sign. When you speak an email address out loud, it is pronounced (using the example above) as 'admin **at** ukwriters dot com'.
3. The 'domain' is usually the name given to a specific computer on the internet. That computer is often your ISP's, but it could also be yours. Each domain is unique on the internet.

4. The 'com' part is the extension that identifies the type of organisation that the address is registered to. Some common extensions are:

.com	a commercial company or corporation
.co.uk	a UK company
.edu	an educational establishment
.gov	a government organisation
.net	a company or organisation in the internet industry

Another rule to remember is that there can be no spaces in an email address. You may sometimes see email addresses with apparent gaps, but the gap will be represented by the underline character _ . For example:

admin@uk_writers.com

If you don't have an email address for someone, or if you think it may be wrong, there is little you can do apart from contact them some other way before trying to email them. There are some email directories on the web, but they are US-biased and contain very few UK entries. They may be worth a try. Here are two well-known ones:

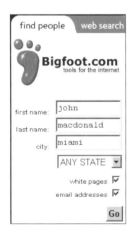

BigFoot
http://www.bigfoot.com

World Email Directory
http://worldemail.com

Email programs

To send and receive emails, you need an email software program ('email client'), such as Outlook Express or Netscape Messenger. Outlook Express is the commonest and easiest one to use. It looks good, and has the advantage of working seamlessly with other Microsoft programs. The second commonest is Netscape Messenger, which comes with the Netscape Navigator package. Both programs are well up to handling your email, and doing lots more useful jobs besides.

You will almost certainly have either Outlook Express or Netscape Messenger installed on your computer. However, you could use a different email client if you wish. Two good and widely-used alternatives are:

Eudora
http://www.eudora.com/light.html

Pegasus Mail
http://www.pegasus.usa.com/current.htm

Writing and reading messages

Email clients let you type in your message and add various kinds of formatting to the page. Some, such as Outlook Express or Netscape Messenger, let you design an email message like a web page. You can

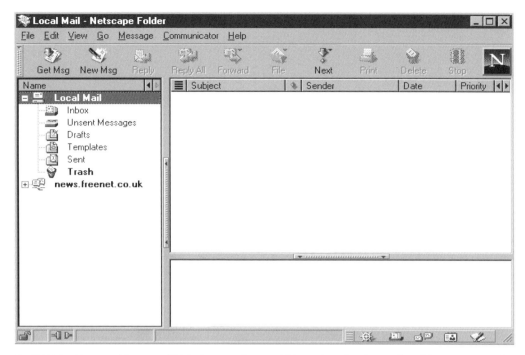

Fig. 27. Using Netscape Messenger. This is the second most widely used email and news client. It is easy to use and well up to the job. It comes as part of the Netscape Communicator set of programs, along with Netscape Navigator and Page Composer.

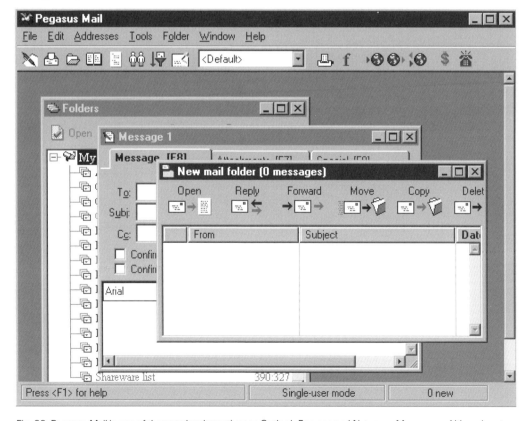

Fig. 28. Pegasus Mail is one of the popular alternatives to Outlook Express and Netscape Messenger. Although not as easy to use, it has some powerful features for managing mailing lists and other automated tasks.

add images, hyperlinks and even sound clips to your message. You can then save your designs as 'stationery' for use in future messages.

You could spend a great deal of time designing and writing email messages, but relax, you don't have to be connected to the internet when writing or reading emails. You only need to be connected when you want to send or receive them. In fact, if you are only interested in email and don't want to browse the web, sending and receiving emails should only take a few seconds, cutting the phone bill right down.

Composing and sending an email message is easy:

1. Open your email client (Outlook Express or Netscape Messenger).
2. Click New Mail (Outlook Express) or New Msg (Netscape Messenger).
3. Insert the email address of the person you want to contact.
4. Compose your message. This part can be as complicated or simple as you want.
5. Click Send.

Smileys

Emails are so easily written and sent that we often send one off before we have had time to digest what we have written. Misunderstandings can easily arise from a careless word in an email message. One of the biggest causes of misunderstanding occurs when people forget that others can't see their facial expression. For example, in a real conversation you would know if a person is only joking, from a smile or a raised eyebrow. In an email message, you cannot see the smile. You would either have to guess or rely on other signs to find out whether a comment was meant seriously or not.

The internet equivalent of body language is the 'smiley':

:)

Tilt your head to the left and you will see a smiling face. Here it is again in a slightly different form:

:-)

That is the basic smiley. You can use it to indicate to people that you are not being serious but joking or making a friendly comment. Make a smiley by typing a colon, a hyphen, then a right bracket. Another form of abbreviated 'body language' is the word 'grin', surrounded by angle brackets: <grin> or <g>.

There is a whole range of smileys and abbreviations for different emotions and situations, and some just for fun. Here are some of them:

:D	laughing
;-)	wink
:-(	frown
:-O	surprise
8-)	wearing glasses
(-:	left-handed person smiling
LOL	laughing out loud

IMO	in my opinion
TIA	thanks in advance
ROTFLMHO	rolling on the floor laughing my head off

Using smileys is fine for personal communications, but they are not usually appropriate in a business setting, unless you know the other person very well.

Checking the email address
To further avoid misunderstandings, always ensure that you are sending the message to the correct email address. Many embarrassing moments have been caused by sending a message to the wrong person. Check the address carefully before you send the message.

Where to look? Every email message includes a 'header'. This is a short piece of text that contains information about where the message is going and who has sent it. The main fields in the header are:

TO: This is where you type the recipient of the message.

CC: This is the 'carbon copy' field where you can specify other people who should also receive copies of the message.

SUBJECT: The subject field should contain a brief description of the content of the message.

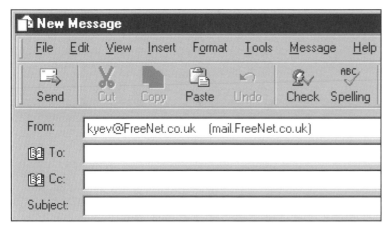

Fig. 29. Email headers. Amongst the information in an email header will be your email address, name, the type of email software you are using, your ISP, and the route that your email message has taken on its journey to the recipient.

Other header fields are included in the email message. For example there are fields containing your name and email address, and which email client you are using. These headers are usually hidden from you by your email client (Outlook Express or Netscape Messenger). These other headers are mostly used to make email more automatic.

Using the Address Book feature
A useful address book facility is available in both Outlook and Messenger. Storing an address in it saves you the bother of having to type it out every time. In Outlook Express, if you want to add a new address, click on Address Book, then New Contact, and type in the details. In Netscape Messenger, click on Address Book, then New Card, and do the same.

Sending and receiving email ···

Sending an email message

After writing a new email message, you click the Send button. If you don't want to go online, the message will be saved in a folder reserved for outgoing mail. In Outlook Express they are saved in the Outbox. In Netscape Messenger they are saved in the Unsent Messages folder. When you next connect to the internet, you can then send all of your email messages in a matter of seconds. At the same time, your email client will check for incoming email messages and retrieve any that are waiting. You can then disconnect and read your new mail offline. You would be surprised at how low your internet telephone bill becomes once you do most of your work offline.

Once mail leaves your computer, it is routed over the internet through a chain of other computers until it reaches the recipient's computer. The process may only take a few seconds. Of course, that person will not receive any messages until he or she connects to the internet. The messages will be stored by their ISP until they do connect. Email is fast but only if you connect to the internet regularly.

Fig. 30. Viewing an incoming email in Outlook Express. The highlighted line in the folder pane on the left shows we are viewing the Inbox (top right pane). The highlighted email there is displayed in the message pane (bottom right).

Dealing with incoming email messages

To receive your email, just connect to the internet and start your email client. Outlook Express and Netscape Messenger will both retrieve your email messages automatically when set up correctly. In fact, you can also set them up to check for new emails periodically while you are online, say browsing the web. Any incoming messages are placed in your inbox or, in Pegasus Mail, the main folder. To read a message, simply double-click on it.

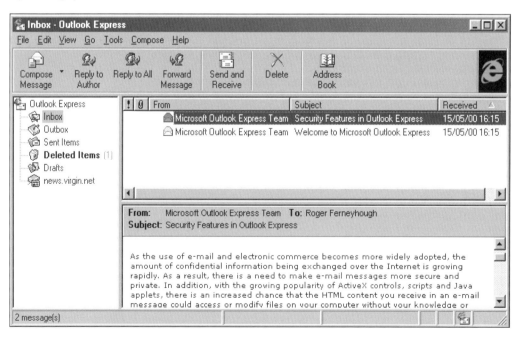

Replying to a message

To reply to a message, open it and click on the Reply button. When you reply to a message, your email client will include the content of the original message in the body of the reply. This is a convention with internet messages. Otherwise, it can become confusing and difficult trying to remember what was written in which email.

If you email a friend and ask 'What is your son's favourite colour?' it may be a few days before she has time to reply. Then, out of the blue, you receive an email with the word 'red' in the message and little else. If you routinely send and receive a number of messages each day, it may take you a while to work out what the 'red' refers to. However, if the reply quoted the original message like:

> > What is your son's favourite colour?
> Red

then there would be no doubt. The › character is the usual way to indicate a line quoted from the received message. Outlook Express uses vertical lines to indicate quoted text. There will be times when replies become more complicated and quoted quotes make an appearance. Look at these two further replies.

> > > What is your son's favourite colour?
> > Red
> What shade?

To which the reply could be:

> > > > What is your son's favourite colour?
> > > Red
> > What shade?
> Manchester United red ;)

Note the multiple use of > by the email clients.

Obviously, you don't have to include all of a message every time, especially if it is a long one. You can just quote the relevant parts and 'snip' out the rest to save space.

Forwarding a message

Forwarding a message is almost identical to replying to one, except that you send it to someone other than the person who sent it. For example, you might want to forward a joke on to another of your friends. When you reply to a message, your email client automatically fills in the email address of the person who sent it. When you forward a message, you must supply the email address of the recipient yourself.

Forwarding a message step by step

1. Select the message you want to forward.
2. Click the Forward button.

3. Fill in the address of the recipient.

4. Add your comments.

5. Click Send.

Managing your messages

Both Outlook Express and Netscape Messenger allow you to create folders very like Windows folders. The folders can also contain sub-folders. To create a new folder in Outlook Express or Netscape Messenger, open the File menu and select New Folder.

Most email clients will also let you sort and save or move messages into different folders and perform automatic filtering to make managing your emails easier (see page 46).

Fig. 31. Using filters in Outlook Express. Filtering incoming email messages can make life far easier when you are trying to separate the many email messages you may soon be getting.

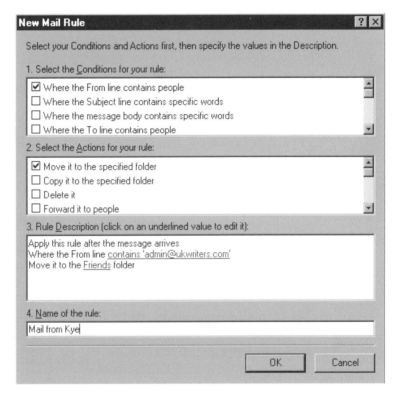

Other Internet Handbooks to help you

Using Email on the Internet

4 Joining in discussion forums

In this chapter we will explore:

▶ *internet mailing lists*

▶ *Usenet: the Hyde Park Corner of the internet*

▶ *using Outlook Express for newsgroups*

▶ *using Netscape Messenger for newsgroups*

▶ *Internet Relay Chat (IRC)*

▶ *web-based chat boards and IRC*

. . . .

Internet mailing lists

Let's extend the email message idea. You can send the same message to a group of people. Just add their addresses to the message and send it to every member of the group. Suppose another person in the group wants to send a reply to the whole group. They can either reply to the original message, or send a new one and include all of the members' email addresses.

Of course, keeping track of everyone's email addresses would need some work. There is a risk that one or more people might forget to include a particular address, and someone could be accidentally left out of future mailings. If the group's membership periodically changes, things can become really confusing, and even disastrous. For example, if you were to send a monthly newsletter to all of the members of your sports club, excluding one of those members may result in an angry resignation or worse.

Suppose instead a single administrator was responsible for membership. Then, everyone could just send messages to the administrator, who would forward them to all the other members. For example, if one member had some sports equipment for sale, she would send the notice to the administrator and it would be forwarded to the other members – no confusion and no lost mail. The administrator would be operating a simple mailing list, probably quite sufficient for a small group of people.

But what if the secretary was on holiday, or sick? The flow of messages would stop – unless you could find a way of doing the work of the administrator automatically. You can, by using a mailing list administrated by a 'list server'.

▶ *Mailing list* – A forum where messages are distributed by email to each member of the forum. There are two types of lists: discussion and announcement. Discussion lists allow exchange between list members. Announcement lists are one-way only and used to distribute information such as news or humour. A good place to find mailing lists is Liszt (http://www.liszt.com). You normally quit a mailing list by sending an email message to request removal.

Fig. 32. The Liszt directory contains links to more than 90,000 different mailing lists. Liszt is a good source if you want to find an email list that covers your favourite topic. Just search for your interest and follow the instructions for subscribing to the list.

▶ *List server* – A computer program that manages a list of members and the flow of messages in a mailing list. The list server is usually installed on the computer system of a permanent organisation like a university or internet service provider.

The administrator of a mailing list keeps a list of members and their email addresses in order to copy and send on all of the messages that come through the mailbox. An internet list server is the same, but instead of just a human administrator, a computer program manages the list of members and the flow of messages. All the human has to do is monitor things. You send a message to the list's email address and it is automatically forwarded to each other person currently on the list.

Joining an internet mailing list
Internet mailing lists are usually free and open to anyone – you don't have to become a member of a club. All you do is ask to be put on the list; in the jargon, you 'subscribe' to the list. There are more than 100,000 different mailing lists on the internet today. They cover almost every conceivable topic, from African-American studies to zone dieting.

Mailing lists are perfect for small and informal groups of people. Unfortunately, when the number of subscribers grows, even mailing lists managed by list servers become unusable. Sending separate (identical) copies of each message to each of the subscribers uses up a lot of internet resources and creates a torrent of messages for people to wade through.

Usenet – the Hyde Park Corner of the internet

Usenet is the internet equivalent of Hyde Park Corner. Over the years, it has grown into a global virtual meeting place. People all over the world can communicate with friends and strangers, discuss events, keep up with news, or talk and gossip about anything that interests them. These discussions are organised by topic in separate forums called 'news-groups'. Each newsgroup consists of a series of messages ('articles' or 'posts').

There are over 80,000 newsgroups in Usenet today. They range from groups created as a joke to serious ones used by large groups of professionals. Almost every hobby or interest has one or more newsgroups dedicated to it. Some newsgroups are inactive and gather cobwebs. Others have hundreds of new messages posted into them every day.

Your newsreader – Outlook Express and/or Netscape Messenger
The messages from an internet mailing list arrive with your normal email messages, but those in newsgroups are handled by a special program called a newsreader. Outlook Express and Netscape Messenger both have newsreaders built into them.

Messages on one particular topic are grouped together and called 'threads'. Threaded messages mean that you can see how a particular discussion progresses as different people reply to the main point.

Unlike mailing list messages, newsgroup articles are stored on your ISP's computer system – their 'news server' – instead of in your mailbox. This way, you only need to fetch the ones that interest you – like newspapers from your local newsagent.

The names of newsgroups
Newsgroups have names that often seem arbitrary and meaningless to outsiders, but they do describe to some extent what kind of topics the group was created for. Newsgroup names are abbreviated descriptions of topics of interest. They consist of a hierarchy of sections separated by dots. For example, there is a newsgroup dedicated to the BBC television soap opera *Eastenders* called:

rec.arts.tv.uk.eastenders

There is another for football called:

uk.sport.football

The 'rec' part of 'rec.arts.tv.uk.eastenders' and the 'uk' part of uk.sport.football' are the top level hierarchies of the newsgroups. The letters 'uk' mean that the group concerns a UK-related topic. Similarly, 'rec' implies a topic to do with recreation. Another top level hierarchy is 'comp' which contains groups discussing computer-related topics.

These broad top level areas are followed by more specific topics such as arts (for art-related topics), sport (for sport subjects), and periphs (for peripherals). So 'comp.periphs' is limited to discussions about computer peripherals – printers, scanners, mice and so on. At a lower level again, the group 'comp.periphs.printers' is limited to discussions about printers.

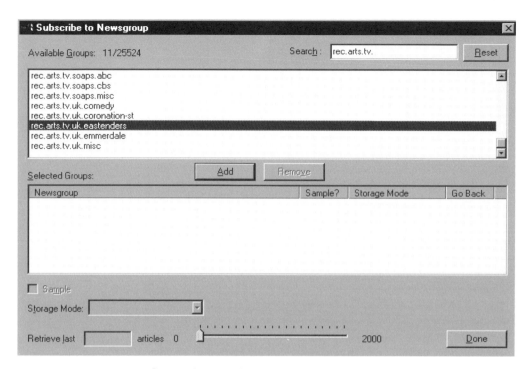

Fig. 33. Subscribing to newsgroups, in this case 'rec.arts.tv.uk.eastenders'. Subscribing to newsgroups does not cost anything and you don't have to register any personal details before you can subscribe – unlike internet mailing lists.

Some other main Usenet hierarchies are:

misc	Discussions that don't fit anywhere else.
net	Usenet II newsgroups (mainly academic).
news	News about Usenet itself.
rec	Hobbies, games and recreation.
sci	Science other than research biology.
soc	'Social' groups, often ethnically related.
talk	Politics and related topics.
uk	Discussions mainly relating to the UK.

Newsgroups may be a wonderful way to share your interests with others but they're often packed with worthless or offfensive postings, many of them anonymous. For this reason alone, you'll eventually need to learn how to use your newsreader to do more than simply download articles. If you intend to use newsgroups for research, you will need a newsreader that can cope. Of the many newsreaders available, Outlook Express is probably the commonest, followed by Netscape Messenger. Both do the job very well.

Starting newsgroups: step by step
Before you can view and take part in newsgroup discussions, you must follow some simple steps:

1. Configure (set up) a news server, and connect to it.
2. Download a list of newsgroups.
3. Subscribe to the ones that interest you.
4. Download the current messages from those groups.

The procedure is similar for both Outlook Express and Netscape Messenger.

Using Outlook Express for newsgroups

Outlook Express is a standard part of Microsoft Windows. It is also included with Internet Explorer installations. Outlook Express is best known for sending and receiving email, but it is also an excellent news-reader. The program is well-organised and easy to use. You can configure the layout to appear as three frames:

▶ Your news server(s) and subscribed groups are shown in the left-hand frame.
▶ Message headers are displayed in the top right frame.
▶ Message contents are displayed in the bottom right frame.

Adding a news server
A news server is a computer that supplies you with a list of newsgroups and current newsgroup articles. Your ISP may well act as your news server, typically giving you access to a (censored or edited) selection of 20,000 to 30,000 newsgroups from the 80,000 or more which exist.

Adding a news server to Outlook Express is easy. There is a wizard that steps you through the process. Select the Tools menu, then

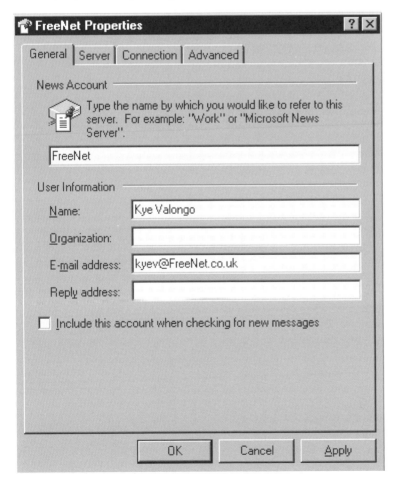

Fig. 34. News properties. When entering your personal details in your news reader, you do not have to use your real name or email address. In fact, it would be unwise to if you intend to use Usenet much. Using your real name and email address will only attract junk mail.

Joining in discussion forums......................................

Accounts, then click on the Add button. Select News, and Outlook Express will start the internet connection wizard. Type in a name and email address for yourself, as you wish them to appear in your articles. Then, enter the correct name of your ISP's news server. For example, if your ISP is Virgin, the news server is called:

news.virgin.net

You can also change your details later if you open the Tools menu and select Accounts. Select the News tab, then double-click on the news server. In this Properties window, you can change server address or any of the other details such as your email address or name.

Downloading a list of newsgroups
Before you can view any newsgroups, you have to download a list of them to your computer. First, click on the news server in the Folders frame. When you highlight the news server, Outlook will ask you if you want to view a list of available newsgroups. If you select 'Yes', Outlook will try to connect to the news server and download this lengthy list. You will need to be patient. Downloading the list may take 10 to 15 minutes, and nothing much may seem to be happening. You will only need to download the list once.

When you add a news server, Outlook Express will prompt you to subscribe to newsgroups on that server. If you prefer, you could subscribe manually later, when you have found a particular newsgroup of interest.

Subscribing to newsgroups
Once you have downloaded the list of newsgroups, subscribing to them is easy. First, highlight the news server in the folders frame on the left of your Outlook Express screen. Then click the Newsgroups button in the preview pane. Select the newsgroup you are interested in and click Subscribe.

You should see something like figure 35. If you now click the Goto button, you will be connected to the internet and Outlook Express will download current articles from that newsgroup – articles posted during the last two or three weeks. You can let it do this, or just click the OK button and download the articles later.

You can cancel your subscription to a newsgroup at any time. Click the Newsgroups button, then the Subscribed tab, select the group, and then click the Unsubscribe button. You can also right-click the newsgroup in the Folders list and then click Unsubscribe.

▶ *Subscribe* – Don't be put off by the words 'subscribe' and 'unsubscribe'. You are under no obligation by subscribing. Access to newsgroups is free and open to anyone, and you can subscribe, unsubscribe, and subscribe again as often as you want, with a click of your mouse.

Searching for newsgroups
You may have trouble scrolling down the thousands of newsgroups to

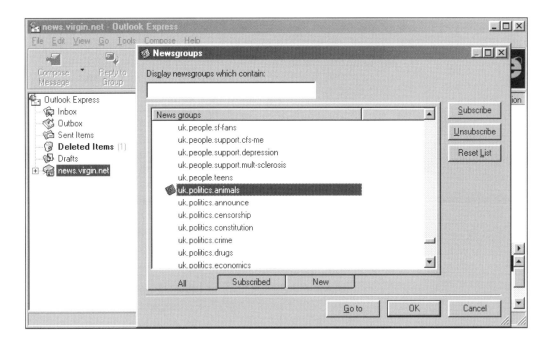

find ones that interest you, so it helps to search for the newsgroup name. To do this, enter a few keywords in the box beneath the line 'Display newsgroups which contain:'

Suppose you are interested in classical guitars. If you know the exact name of the newsgroup you want – 'rec.music.classical.guitar' for example – you would type in that exact phrase. If you are unsure of the name of the group, you can just enter 'guitar'. Entering 'guitar' brings up a list of about twenty different groups with the word 'guitar' in their name. Highlight the group you want and click the Subscribe button. Click OK. You will see that the group name now appears in the Folder window underneath the server name. You can also double-click a name in the Newsgroup list to subscribe.

Fig. 35. A list of newsgroups supplied by a news server (news.virgin.net), and displayed in Outlook Express. It is a very long A to Z list. Here are just a few of the UK newsgroups in the list. To view messages in a newsgroup, highlight its name, and click Subscribe.

Fig. 36. Subscribing to a newsgroup. You can subscribe to as many or as few newsgroups as you wish. The more you do, the more articles you will end up reading. This person has just subscribed to one newsgroup. To remove it, click Unsubscribe on the right.

Joining in discussion forums ....

Downloading and reading articles

To download articles from a newsgroup, make sure you are connected to the internet. Then, just click on the newsgroup's name in the Folders window. Outlook will then download any new articles from the news server and display them in the preview pane (top right pane).

Outlook Express has a 'synchronise' feature. It downloads the articles and subject lines from all of your subscribed groups in one go. Usually, Outlook Express will only download the subject lines ('headers') but you can configure it to download the whole body of the article when you select the group. To do this, select the newsgroup, open the File menu and select Properties. Click the Synchronise tab and check 'When synchronising this newsgroup, download:' and select one of:

1. New headers.
2. New messages (Headers and bodies).
3. All messages (Headers and bodies).

Now click OK and then click the Synchronise button.

Fig. 37. Downloading and reading articles in Outlook Express. The news server is 'news.virgin.net' and the newsgroup is called 'uk.politics.animals'. The message headers are displayed in the top right pane, and the highlighted message in the bottom right.

Posting and replying to messages

There are several ways that you can post messages, depending on whether you are posting a new message or replying to one.

In the Folders list, select the newsgroup you want to post a message to. To post a new article, click the New Post button. Enter the Subject of your article, write the message you want to send, then click the Send button.

To cross-post your message to multiple newsgroups, click the icon next to Newsgroups in the New Message dialog box before you click on

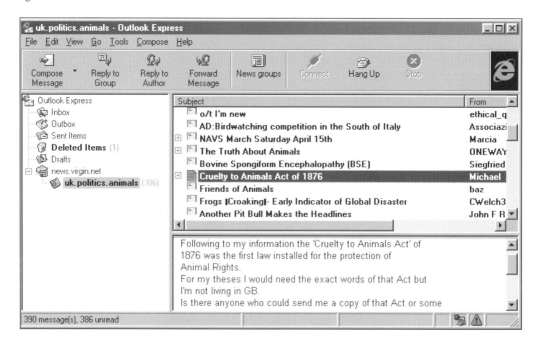

the Send button. In the Pick Newsgroups dialog box, select the newsgroups from the list, and then click Add. Remember, though, if you send the same message to many newsgroups, people may complain to your ISP and in serious cases they may terminate your account.

You may want to cancel a message you have posted. Select the message once it has appeared in the newsgroup, click the Message menu, and then select Cancel Message.

Filtering articles and email messages
Outlook Express lets you define multiple filters to screen your incoming newsgroup articles and emails. They can be based on who the message was sent by, how old it is, the size, and what the subject line contains. If the message is from a newsgroup, it says which one it is from. You can also combine rules in many ways such as:

1. where the 'from' line contains 'Kye Valongo'
2. AND the 'subject' line contains 'Internet Handbooks'
3. mark the message for download.

Outlook calls filters 'rules'. You can use rules to mark certain messages, highlight messages in colour, have certain messages downloaded, or even delete unwanted messages before you see them.

To create a rule, open the Tools menu, select Message Rules, and click News (or Mail if you want to create an email filter). On the News Rules tab, click New. Select the conditions for your rule by checking or clearing the check boxes in the Conditions section – for example 'Where the

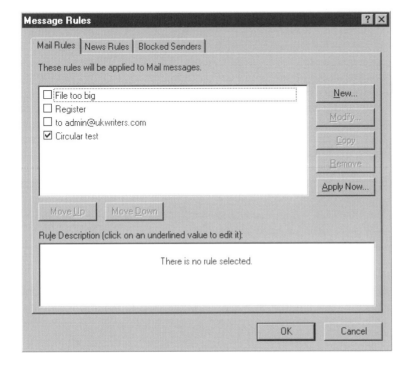

Fig. 38. Newsgroup rules. Setting up filtering rules for your newsgroup articles will help you to separate out the really important messages from the inevitable junk mail and routing messages.

From line contains people'. You can also specify multiple conditions for a single rule by clicking more than one check box.

Click the hyperlinks in the Rule Description section – in this case, the underlined text contains people – to fill in the details of your rule (in this case, to select a person). If you have more than one condition, you can also specify whether all the rule conditions must be met (and), or whether at least one must be met (or).

In the Name of the rule box, type new name for your rule, and then click OK. The next time you download articles from the newsgroup, these filters will take effect.

Using Netscape Messenger for newsgroups

Messenger is part of the Netscape Communicator suite. Like Outlook Express, it deals with both email and Usenet quite adequately. As in Outlook Express, you need to specify your news server, probably supplied by your internet service provider. For example, if you use Virgin, your news server is called:

news.virgin.net

You must then download the lengthy list of 20,000 to 30,000 newsgroups before you can do anything else. Annoyingly, Communicator does not indicate the progress when downloading this important list, other than to say 'Retrieving discussion groups'. You may think the program has crashed, since it just sits there apparently doing nothing. Don't worry, just wait 10 to 15 minutes and the very long list will suddenly appear in a rush.

Configuring your news server
Open the Edit menu then select Preferences. In the Mail and Newsgroups section, select Newsgroup servers. You will see the server address in the pane on the right – you cannot change this without deleting the server and then adding a new one. To set up your name and email address, in the Mail and Newsgroups section, select Identity.

To add a news server, click Add or to modify the information, click Edit. To remove a server: click Delete. At the Newsgroup folder, type in the path name of a local folder where your newsgroup server can download messages. For example:

C:\Program Files\Netscape\Communicator\News

Then click 'OK'. When you next connect to the internet, Messenger will download the list of newsgroups. (Note: you do not need to provide the name of a news folder on computers with Mac OS.)

Subscribing to newsgroups
Highlight the news server and click the right mouse button. Select 'Subscribe to newsgroups'. In the 'Subscribe to newsgroups' window, find and select the newsgroups you are interested in and click the 'Subscribe' button. Messenger uses folders to organise the newsgroups, so you may

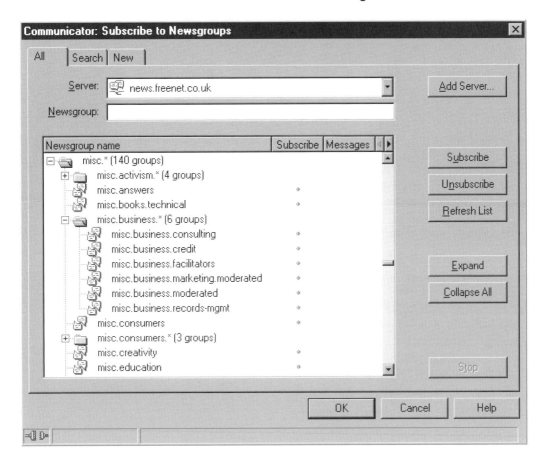

Fig. 39. A list of newsgroups displayed in the Netscape Communicator newsreader. Outlook displays thousands of them A to Z (figure 35) but Netscape displays them under subject hierarchies. Click to highlight any one that appeals to you, then click Subscribe.

have to click to open the folders and dig around a little. If you are connected to the internet, Messenger will try to download a list of newsgroups; if you are not connected (offline), you will be shown a list of newsgroup names that were previously downloaded.

For example to find the group rec.music.classical.guitar, you have to open the 'rec' folder, then 'rec.music', then 'rec.music.classical'. Select rec.music.classical.guitar from the list and click the Subscribe button. Alternatively, you could go to the Search tab and type in rec.music.classical.guitar to find the group, then click on the Subscribe button.

Downloading and reading articles

To download articles in a newsgroup, connect to the internet then simply click on the newsgroup. Messenger will automatically download the subject lines of any articles not already stored on your computer. If you click on any message, the text of the message will be downloaded and will appear in the message pane.

You can view message headers in their respective threads, and sort them by a combination of criteria, mark and unmark headers, tag others for later retrieval, post replies, and of course send email directly to another person.

57

Joining in discussion forums...

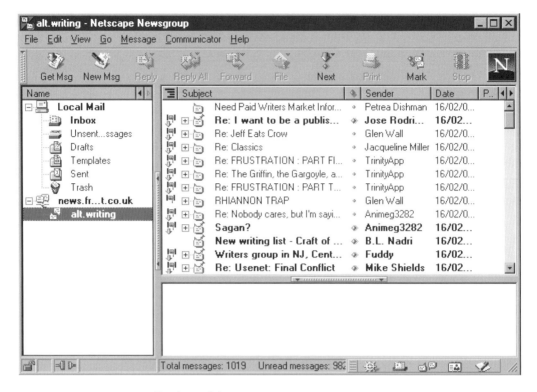

Fig. 40. Reading

Fig. 40. Reading newsgroup articles in Netscape Communicator. When you have selected a newsgroup, such as 'alt.writing', the right-hand pane displays the article headers, and the bottom pane will show the content of any article you click to highlight.

Posting articles

(a) To post a newsgroup article using Messenger, simply select the newsgroup in the folders pane on the left of the screen, and press the New Msg button. To reply to an existing article, press the Reply button and choose 'to Newsgroup'. To reply to the group and also send an email message to the individual, click Reply All and choose 'to Sender and Group'.

(b) To cancel an article that you have posted, right-click on the message and select Cancel Message.

(c) To cross post: highlight one of the newsgroups in your subscribed groups list and click the New Msg button. Then, in the top line of the new message, where you see the first newsgroup name, type in the other newsgroup names separated by commas. Click the Send button.

Filtering articles and email messages

To apply filters to newsgroups, open the Edit menu and select Message Filters. Select the relevant newsgroup from the list of groups below 'Filters for' and click New. Filtering in Messenger is very much like filtering in Outlook Express.

Internet Relay Chat (IRC)

Chatting is one of the most popular social activities on the internet.

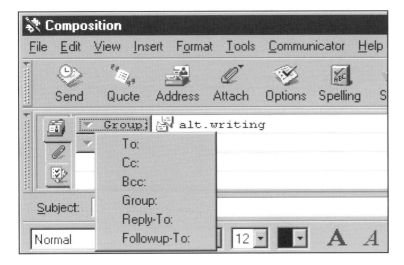

Fig. 41. Posting an article using Netscape Communicator. When doing this, you can send a copy to someone by email (cc) or a blind copy (bcc). The latter excludes the email address of the recipient from the newsgroup article header. With cc, it would be included.

Indeed, it is one of the big selling features of online services such as America OnLine. 'Chatting' is done using nicknames or 'nicks'. Real names are rarely used, so you can never be sure about the person you are chatting to. 'Little Sally' may be burly Frank in real life. The risk of being deceived is high, so although you can relax and have fun, trust no one.

Internet Relay Chat is the original chat medium on the internet. It is still the most widely used means of chatting with people. IRC exists globally, and it is estimated that more than 100,000 people are online chatting at any one time.

IRC is a multi-user chat system, where people meet on channels to talk in groups, or privately. Chats are conducted by typing sentences to one another on the channel. You type 'hello' for instance, and someone else might type 'hi, how are you?'. And so the conversation goes on.

These typed messages are passed around by IRC servers. One server can be connected to several other servers on any one of various IRC networks, large and small.

How to join IRC
To participate in an IRC chat, you will need to:

1. download an IRC program (called an IRC client)
2. connect to an IRC server
3. join a chat channel
4. type away

Two good widely-used IRC clients are Mirc and Pirch. Download either, and you will not be disappointed:

Mirc
ftp://oak.oakland.edu/pub/irc/

Pirch
http://www.bcpl.lib.md.us/~frappa/pirch.html

Joining in discussion forums...

Fig. 42. The Mirc chat client. Mirc is the most popular IRC program by far. It is easy to use but also includes many features for the more advanced user.

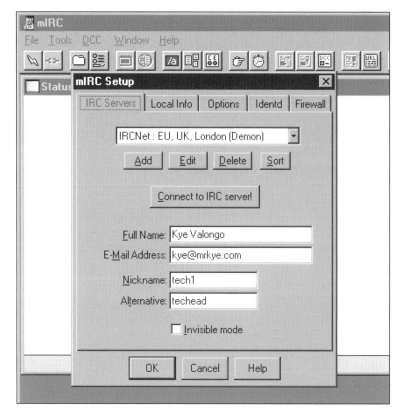

The first time you run your IRC client, you will be asked to fill in some information about yourself such as your name, email address, and nickname.

You will then be able to choose a server to connect to IRC. It's usually best to connect to a geographically close server from the list. On IRC you will be known to others by your nickname or 'nick'. Choose any nickname you like. But make it less than 9 characters long and don't use spaces or unusual characters. If you come across another person using the same nick, you may be asked to switch to another one to avoid confusion.

To join conversations and send private messages you need to learn some simple commands. All of the commands start with a forward slash, the '/' character. Anything that does not begin with '/' is assumed to be a message to someone and will be sent to the others on the channel. The most common commands on IRC are:

/HELP	Show general help or help on the given command.
/LIST	List all current channels.
/JOIN	Join a channel.
/PART	Leave a channel (also /LEAVE).
/QUIT	Exit your IRC session, (also /BYE and /EXIT).
/NICK	Change your nickname.
/TOPIC	Change the topic of the channel.
/AWAY	Leave a message saying you're away from your computer.

Various other commands have to do with others on the channel:

/WHOIS   Display information about someone.
/INVITE   Send an invitation to another user.
/MSG   Send a private message.

These are used with the person's nick placed after the command. For example:

/MSG teddy1

This starts a private conversation between you and the person nick-named teddy1.

Now you are ready to get started: click on the 'connect' button and wait for the server to respond. You will get an introductory message from the server and then informed that you are logged on. Now give the /list command and prepare to wait for a couple of minutes until the list of channels loads.

Next, before you can start any conversation, you must join a channel. To do this, find one that sounds interesting and type:

/join #channelname

Fig. 43. The Pirch chat client. Joining the IRC help channel is easy. Just type /join #irchelp then press the enter key. You will probably join in the middle of a conversation so just type 'hello' and watch the conversation develop for a few seconds.

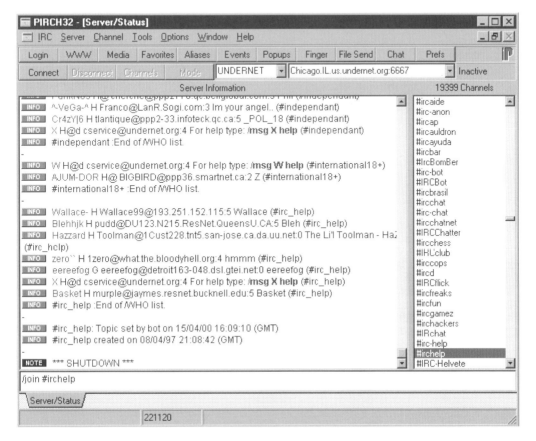

Joining in discussion forums ....

Try '/join #irchelp' which is a channel for IRC beginners. Often the channel name has nothing to do with the conversation that is going on in the channel, but you will soon get a feel for which ones are for you.

When you give the /join command, a second window opens: the channel window, in which you'll see on the right-hand side a list of people who are already there.

You will almost always join a channel in the middle of a conversation. It's a good plan to watch the conversation for a minute or two. When you are ready to start talking, just type your words, a line at a time, remembering to press the return or Enter key. Start with a simple 'hello!' then wait for a few seconds. There is often a delay because you may be talking to someone on the other side of the world. You will soon become part of a conversation – enjoy yourself but be careful about giving away personal information.

Fig. 44. The IRC help channel. Once you are on the channel, you will see the conversation unfold. The list on the right shows the weird and wonderful nicknames of other users on the channel. Join in when you feel comfortable.

When you want to leave a channel, just type /part #channelname. Remember to disconnect your internet connection when you have finished.

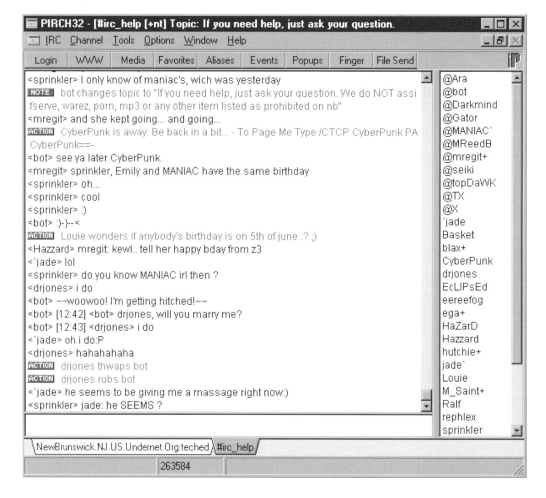

62

Web-based chat boards and IRC

On the world wide web, you can also chat to other people on special web sites. The experience is very similar to IRC, but there are few if any commands to worry about, and there are fewer topics. In some cases, a private chat can be arranged between two parties who meet initially in a group chat. Many chats are focused on a particular topic of interest relevant to the web site. Some involve guest experts or famous people who 'talk' to anyone involved in the chat.

Here are some good web-based chat rooms to explore:

Chatway
http://www.chatway.com/

Chat Planet
http://www.chatplanet.com/

Excite Talk
http://talk.excite.com/communities/chat/home/

OmniChat
http://www.4-lane.com/

SneakerChat
http://www.sneakerchat.com/

Talk City
http://www.talkcity.com/

Other Internet Handbooks to help you

Chat & Chat Rooms on the Internet
Discussion Forums on the Internet

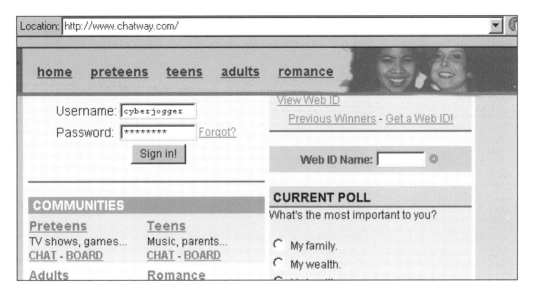

5 Pictures and games: downloading and swapping files

In this chapter we will explore:

▶ *downloading files from the web*

▶ *sending and receiving files by email*

▶ *free games and other programs*

▶ *pictures on the net*

Downloading files from the web

Fig. 45. The Nonags free software web site. Being able to find and download free software is one of the advantages of having an internet connection. Be careful, though, because downloaded software is one of the main sources of virus infection.

Not all sites that you come across on the web are web sites. Some are file archives. These store files of all types from games to academic information and financial packages. These archive sites are called FTP servers. FTP stands for file transfer protocol.

When your browser visits one of these sites, it changes its behaviour a little. It becomes more like Windows Explorer than a web browser; you can copy files to and from the FTP server just as you can on your own computer. Most servers, however, will not let you copy any files onto their server unless you have special permission.

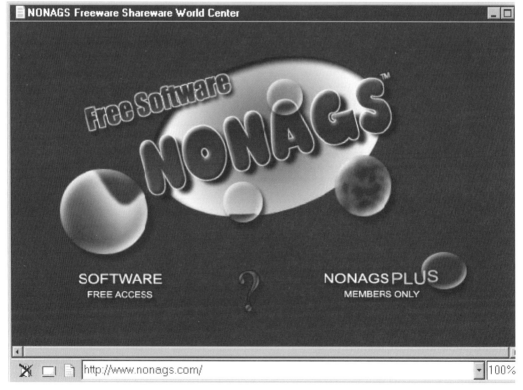

.... Pictures and games: downloading and swapping files

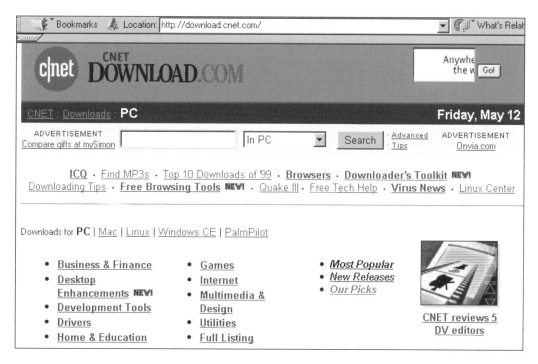

There are lots of public FTP archives that let you log on and search for files by category.

Here are some of the better known ones:

Download.com
http://download.cnet.com/

Simtel.net
http://www.simtel.net/simtel.net/

Tucows
http://www.tucows.com/

Nonags
http://www.nonags.com/

Be extremely careful with downloaded programs. Always check them for viruses before you run them. See page 81 for more information on viruses.

Compressed files
Many files for downloading are electronically compressed. This way they can be uploaded or downloaded more quickly across the internet, saving everybody time and money. If an image file is compressed too much, there may be a loss of quality. To read such files you need to uncompress ('unzip' or 'unpack') them. A good first FTP site to visit is WinZip:

ftp://208.240.94.167/winzip70.exe

Fig. 46. Download.Com is an excellent and massive source of free software downloads. All kinds of useful software programs are available for everyone.

Pictures and games: downloading and swapping files................

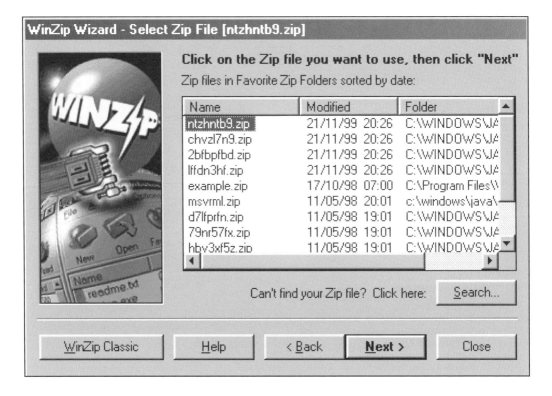

WinZip Wizard - Select Zip File [ntzhntb9.zip]

Click on the Zip file you want to use, then click "Next"

Zip files in Favorite Zip Folders sorted by date:

Name	Modified	Folder
ntzhntb9.zip	21/11/99 20:26	C:\WINDOWS\JA
chvzl7n9.zip	21/11/99 20:26	C:\WINDOWS\JA
2bfbpfbd.zip	21/11/99 20:26	C:\WINDOWS\JA
lffdn3hf.zip	21/11/99 20:26	C:\WINDOWS\JA
example.zip	17/10/98 07:00	C:\Program Files\\
msvrml.zip	11/05/98 20:01	c:\windows\java\
d7lfprfn.zip	11/05/98 19:01	C:\WINDOWS\JA
79nr57fx.zip	11/05/98 19:01	C:\WINDOWS\JA
hbv3xf5z.zip	11/05/98 19:01	C:\WINDOWS\JA

Can't find your Zip file? Click here: [Search...]

[WinZip Classic] [Help] [< Back] [Next >] [Close]

Fig. 47. WinZip is a basic software utility, and well worth getting. It enables you to open ('unzip') and use any programs sent to you in a compressed ('zipped') format.

This will download the installation file for its popular and freely available program, WinZip. This is an essential and easy-to-use program for everyone who intends to download files. WinZip will decompress files that you download from FTP sites, and it will compress files should you need to. For more information see its web site:

WinZip
http://www.winzip.com/

Sending and receiving files by email

As well as sending simple messages, you can also send and receive files such as documents, sounds, images or even whole games by email. You simply attach them to normal email messages. Files attached to email messages are called, of course, attachments. You can send and receive any kind of file, but there are two points to keep in mind when sending files:

1. Large files take a long time to send and receive.

2. The recipient of your attachment may not be able to use the type of file you are sending. For example, if you attach a Lotus spreadsheet, he may not be able to view it unless he has Lotus software installed on his computer.

3. Some files such as images or video clips can be very large and will take hours to send. More importantly, they will also take hours for the recipient to download at the other end. If the attachment is not really important, you may really annoy that person. Remember, they may have to pay for telephone time. A large file – that they might not want anyway – may cost them several pounds to download. Before you send those cute family pictures, check their size – something over one megabyte could take up more than an hour of telephone time. And although you send it off-peak, the recipient may connect at peak rate and thus pay much more.

Sending attachments with your emails
Most email clients such as Outlook Express and Netscape Messenger handle attachments in the same way:

1. Create a new email message in the normal way.

2. Click the 'Attach' button or tab.

3. Select the file you want to send.

4. Repeat the process if you want to attach more than one file to your email message.

5. Click the 'Send' button.

Fig. 48. Sending an attached file with an email in Outlook Express. File attachments are a great way to share information with people. But note that the recipient may not wish to waste a lot of time downloading a large file that he or she did not ask for in the first place.

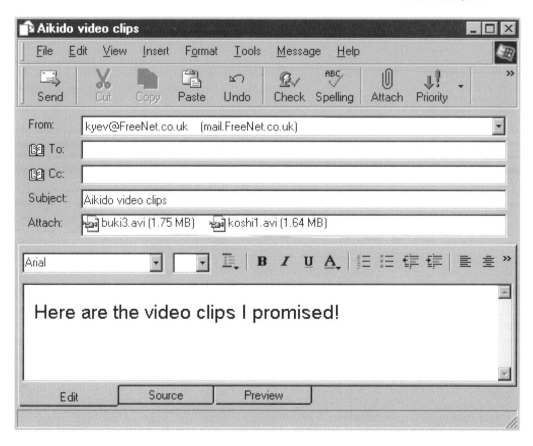

Pictures and games: downloading and swapping files...............

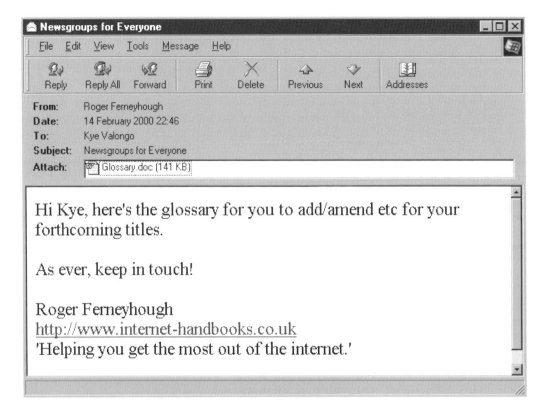

Fig. 49. An incoming attachment, in this case a text file called Glossary. Retrieving attachments in an email message can take time so it's best do it at off-peak times if you can. Be careful when opening or running attached files. Check them for viruses first.

Receiving and opening attachments

You receive an attachment just as you would a normal email message, but usually it takes longer to download. Double-click the name of the attachment (in this case Glossary.doc) to open it or save it to disk. You may not, however, be able to open the attachment if you don't have the software program associated with it. For example, if you do not have Microsoft Word, you may not be able to open a Word document. The same goes for other programs.

Email messages with attachments pose one of the worst virus threats to home PC user, so before you dabble with attachments see page 81 to learn more about viruses. Also, see the book *Your Privacy on the Internet* in this series.

Free games and other programs

There is rarely anything free that does not have a hidden catch. Well, the internet has a surprising amount of useful free stuff that does come without a catch. The usual catch with free software is that it is limited to a section of the full program, but at least that section is fully working. The developer's hope is that you will like the program so much that you will buy the full version.

Games are often given away as demo programs. They allow you to play one or two levels of the game to try it out. These trials are called shareware. Other shareware programs give you full functionality, but nag you with reminders asking you to pay for the registered version (which will not nag you!)

▶ *Shareware* – Software that you can try before you buy. Usually there is some kind of limitation to the game such as a time limit, or limited features. To get the registered version, you must pay for the software.

A good source of shareware is:

FilePile.Com
http://img.filepile.com
FilePile is the world's largest indexed collection of shareware files. It has a staggering million-plus free software programs you can download free. They cover all platforms of computer operating systems including applications, games and pictures.

Pictures on the net

The first thing most people think of when they think of pictures on the internet is pornography. There is certainly a good deal of that, but there are also millions of 'proper' pictures as displayed in the world's great art galleries. The world's largest and most comprehensive archive which is devoted to images of painting, sculpture and architecture is:

Artres
http://www.artres.com
You can gain access to more than 3 million images on the site. Some other picture archives online are:

The Louvre, Paris   http://mistral.culture.fr/louvre/louvre
The Electric Gallery   http://www.egallery.com/index.html
British Journal of Photography   http://www.bjphoto.co.uk

Downloading an image step-by-step
This is simplicity itself. When viewing a web site with an image you want to save on your computer:

1. Right-click on the image.
2. In Internet Explorer, select 'Save picture as'. In Netscape, select 'Save image as'.
3. Type in a name for the image.
4. Select a location, in other words highlight the folder or drive where you want to store it.
5. Click 'Save'.

If you want the image to act as your desktop wallpaper, it is even easier:

(a) Right-click the image.

(b) Select 'Set as wallpaper'.

Minimise your programs and admire the new picture on your desktop.

If you plan to use an image for more than your own pleasure, though, you should ask permission of the artist or owner of the image. Although the image has been published on the internet, it may still leave you open to legal action should you use the image, or any text for that matter, in any public medium. You may think that a picture of the Mona Lisa would brighten up your newsletter or web site but you may end up in court. If in doubt, ask.

Porn

Speaking of pornography, most countries have laws restricting the creation and possession of pornography, including on personal computers. The legal definitions and scope of pornography vary a good deal from one country to another. Technically, as soon as you view a site with images, you have those images on your computer. Where? – in your browser's temporary storage area called the cache.

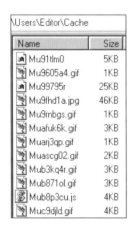

The cache

Your cache is designed to speed up your online browsing by saving much of a site's content on your hard drive. This idea is that when you visit the same site, you don't have to download the same content again. If you want to be sure that illegal images are not kept on your computer, you should clear the cache. It may slow down your next few surfing sessions, but not for long.

Emptying your cache in Internet Explorer

1. Open the Tools menu.

2. Choose Internet options.

3. In the temporary internet files section, click the Delete Files button.

4. When you are asked if you want to delete your offline content, click the check box to place a tick in it.

5. Click OK.

6. Then click OK again to close the Internet Options window.

Emptying your cache in Netscape Navigator

1. Open the Edit menu.

2. Choose Preferences.

3. Double-click the Advanced category to open it.

4. Select Cache.

5. Click the Clear Disk Cache button then click OK.

6. Click the Clear Memory Cache button then click OK.

Deletion of files

It is a common misconception that deleting a file on a computer removes it for good. 'Delete' does not in fact mean delete. 'Delete' merely removes

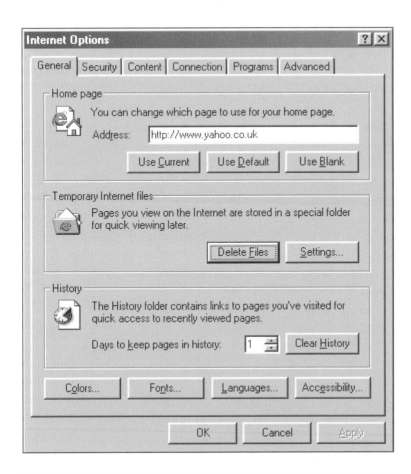

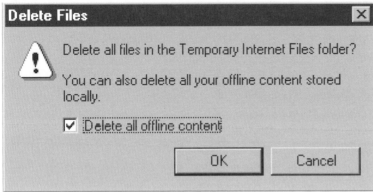

Fig. 50. Deleting your temporary internet files. Internet Explorer and Netscape both save the web pages you have viewed, in part of the hard drive called the cache. Emptying the cache might save you from an unpleasant interview or court appearance one day.

Pictures and games: downloading and swapping files...............

part of the filename, and the file from view, but the file itself will remain on the hard disk until overwritten by some other file. Inexpensive computer tools such as Norton Utilities can easily recover 'deleted' files on a computer. To permanently remove unwanted files from your computer requires the use of software which provides secure deletion by repeated overwriting of the selected files.

Other Internet Handbooks to help you

Your Privacy on the Internet

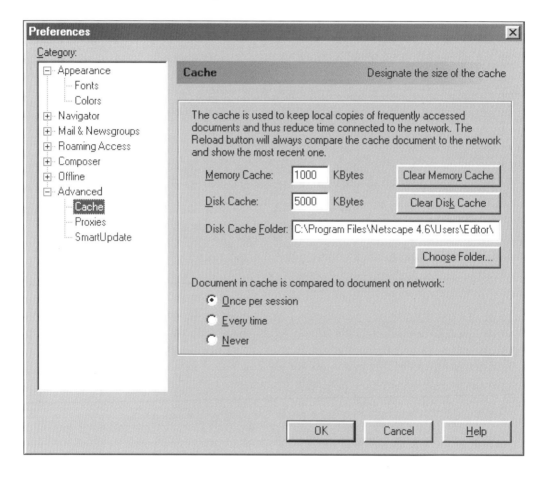

Preferences ☒

Category:

- ☐ Appearance
  - Fonts
  - Colors
- ☐ Navigator
- ☐ Mail & Newsgroups
- ☐ Roaming Access
- ☐ Composer
- ☐ Offline
- ☐ Advanced
  - Cache
  - Proxies
  - SmartUpdate

Cache   Designate the size of the cache

The cache is used to keep local copies of frequently accessed documents and thus reduce time connected to the network. The Reload button will always compare the cache document to the network and show the most recent one.

Memory Cache: `1000` KBytes   [Clear Memory Cache]

Disk Cache: `5000` KBytes   [Clear Disk Cache]

Disk Cache Folder: `C:\Program Files\Netscape 4.6\Users\Editor\`

[Choose Folder...]

Document in cache is compared to document on network:

- ⦿ Once per session
- ○ Every time
- ○ Never

[OK] [Cancel] [Help]

6 Internet risks and remedies

In this chapter we will explore:

▶ *risks for internet shoppers*
▶ *protecting your personal privacy*
▶ *protecting children online*
▶ *protecting yourself against computer viruses*

Risks for internet shoppers

Buying things on the net

Buying things on the internet is easy, but it can be risky. There are many less-than-honest web sites out there. Many con artists who have used other media to feed on victims are moving online. It is so easy for anyone to construct a professional-looking site, and it is becoming harder to know for sure whether a site is reliable. You can trust big name sites such as Tesco or Waterstones, but what about the thousands of smaller specialised sites such as one which advertises secretarial services, or family-tree tracing services?

Avoiding online cons

Here are some ways to avoid being conned when buying products on the internet:

1. Only supply your credit card details over a secure server. You can tell if the connection is secure in these ways:
    –   The URL of the order page may begin with https:// rather than just http://
    –   Your browser should display a message saying that you are entering a secure zone.
2. Ring the phone number on the web site if possible, to make sure the organisation is genuine.

Fig. 51. The security notice in Internet Explorer. This pops up in your browser window when you are about to enter a secure web site, such as an online shop which uses special security technology to safeguard credit card transactions.

Internet risks and remedies..

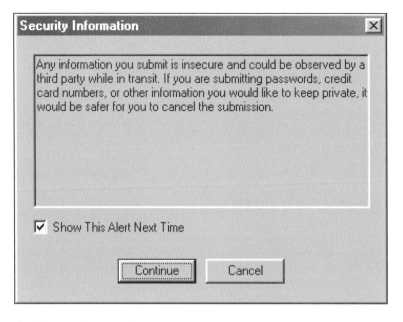

3. Print and keep copies of your order. It is too easy to forget the vital details, which may be needed if it comes to a dispute.

4. If the offer is too good to be true, it probably is especially if it promises some kind of miraculous cure or easy money. Wherever possible check the facts and ask or read about their returns policy.

5. Check your next credit card statement. If you see a problem, inform your credit card company immediately. It can wield a lot of power, including overseas.

6. Consult the Advertising Standards Agency and Office of Fair Trading and search for any complaints about the company that you are thinking of paying:

   http://www.open.gov.uk/oft/frames/consumer.htm

7. Be extra careful when buying from overseas companies. UK laws probably don't apply and you may not have any protection.

8. Never give anyone your dial-up password. If you need a password to buy something or set up an account, create a different one.

9. Pay attention to the accuracy of information you enter when placing your order. Be careful to make sure that the quantity, price, availability and shipping charges are acceptable to you. Be wary of companies that ask you to supply unnecessary information, such as your bank account numbers.

10. Ask these questions:
    - How long has the company been in business?
    - What are its return policies?
    - What will it do with the personal information you give them (credit card number, address, phone number, email address)?

Many of these questions can be emailed to contact the firm you're considering using. This is also a good way to see how quickly they respond to emails – useful if you need help or support later.

Protecting your personal privacy

Clear those Usenet archives

We may not realise it when we post messages to Usenet but it is probably the most public place on the internet. Anybody can compile a dossier on you from your posts. In fact there are companies that specialise in collecting every post on Usenet. Deja (http://www.deja.com) is one such company that makes the information available to all who visit its site. Go to the site and enter a search with my name – Kye Valongo – and you'll be surprised at how much you can find out about me.

Posting History: admin@ukwriters.com (Kye Valongo)

There are 135 unique messages by
admin@ukwriters.com (Kye Valongo)   **Get all 135 messages**
(numbers may be slightly skewed by cross-postings)

Number of Messages	Forum
49	uk.net.news.config
41	uk.culture.arts.writing
17	alt.writing
5	uk.media
3	uk.media.newspapers
3	york.fes.writers-cafe
2	alt.skunks
2	comp.society.privacy
1	uk.rec.cars.4x4
1	uk.rec.motorcycles

Fig. 53. A message poster's profile in Deja. Viewing a profile like this enables you to find out quite a lot about someone. This one tells you something about the author's taste in cars, security, possible political preferences, and personality quirks.

Anything you post to a newsgroup will be recorded for a very long time at sites like Deja. With this in mind, the only way to prevent your posts from being archived is to say nothing. But there are times when you just have to speak out. So, how can you minimise the amount of information that is kept?

You can prevent your posts from being stored by adding the text 'x-no-archive:yes' to the headers of your outgoing messages. To do this in Outlook Express, type in 'x-no-archive:yes' as the *first* line of the message. It will not work if it comes later in the message. Using this header ensures that when services such as Deja scan the Usenet posts, yours will not be archived. However, if somebody includes your text when they reply to your post, your words may be stored in the archive as part of that others person's messages. Is there a way around this? Only one: say nothing that you would not want on permanent public record.

Internet risks and remedies...

No matter how innocent and neutral your posts to Usenet are, your privacy will still end up being abused. Junk mailers use archives like Deja and also scan the newsgroups themselves to harvest email addresses. All it needs is one post and you will become a target: your email address will be in hundreds of junk mail databases.

Protecting children online

Few cases of child abuse resulting from the internet have appeared in the news. However, incidents may go unreported if children feel unable to discuss them with parents. Children can become involved in many types of harmful incidents: from being tricked into revealing information about their personal life to something as serious as kidnapping and sexual abuse. The internet gives disturbed people the confidence to do or say things that would be impossible in a normal social environment.

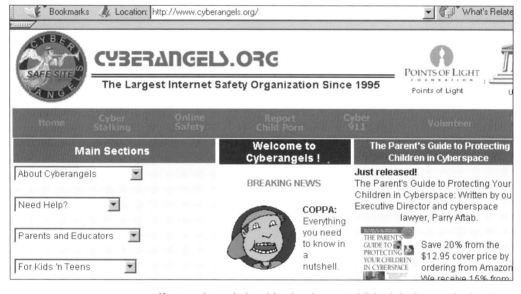

Fig. 54. Cyberangels is one of various useful sites on the web that deal with risks to children. Take a look around and read what they have to say before you let your children loose on the internet without supervision.

If a trusting relationship develops, a child might be manipulated or tricked into providing personal information or arranging a meeting that might result in danger to the child or family members. In some cases, children have been tricked through email, bulletin boards, or chat areas. Paedophiles have been known to use alternative identities to gain a child's confidence then arrange a face-to-face meeting.

There is also the risk of a child being tricked into doing something that has negative legal or financial consequences. Children may unwittingly give out a credit card number – yours maybe – or do something that is illegal in some way. If the child is using your email account, you may be the one in court for libel or worse. For example, many would-be hackers are teenagers who fail to realise the risks of what they are doing. At the very least, a careless word here or there may result in legal action being taken against you or your child.

These are worst-case situations, but make no mistake, there are serious threats to your children out there on the internet. What child can resist having some secrets from their parents? Your child may think that the secret friend is a 16-year-old, but are they? Take this imaginary scenario as a warning. It is set in an internet chat room.

Trudy: Hi there!
John: Hello
Trudy: Where do you live?
John: Ashton, what about you
Trudy: Hey, I live there too, on Church Street, what street are you on?
John: Market Street, number 25
Trudy: Cool!

It sounds innocent enough, doesn't it? But a Church street can be found in almost any town and what if 'Trudy' was in fact a 50-year-old male paedophile? Would you realise that a paedophile had actually gained access directly to your child's bedroom (where many children's computers are)?

What can you do?
Remember, if your child has a computer in their room, it stops being merely a computer as soon as it is connected to the internet. It becomes a kind of doorway that practically anyone in the world can use to penetrate your home environment via your child's bedroom. Would you allow a stranger to enter your child's bedroom without your knowledge?

There are three main ways you can protect your children:

1. Use blocking software. This gives access to the web, but monitors the connection and filters out any sites containing keywords you have specified as undesirable.

2. Enable the ratings system in your browser (see below). This uses information about the content of a site to decide whether it is acceptable or not. The unacceptable sites are filtered out.

3. Parental guidance and education. For example, only allow the use of the computer in a communal area such as the kitchen where people are likely to be around.

Both blocking software and the rating systems are forms of censorship, and as adults many of us would object strongly to any form of censorship. It might be possible that the internet is the only place a child can find information, advice and support. Children who have become drug users or may be gay, or have problems of some other kind, will find the support they need on the internet – many of the filtering systems will deny them access to these important sites.

Of course, many children know already how to crack the software so that they can bypass the filters. And once one child has cracked the software, the know-how will quickly spread to children all over the world. You can see for yourself by visiting a site set up by an American teenager, called Peacefire:

Peacefire
http://www.peacefire.org

How to disable:
• CYBERsitter
• Cyber Patrol
• SurfWatch
• Net Nanny
Research material

Fig. 55. Surfmonkey is 'the web for kids'. It is an entertaining area offering a censored experience of the internet for children. The browser itself takes on the guise of a spaceship that the child can use to splat or explode web sites.

Filtering software

1. *Netnanny* (http://www.netnanny.com) – Net Nanny blocks or screens unsuitable material. It also prevents your address, phone and credit card numbers from being given out over the internet.

2. *SurfMonkey* (http://www.surfmonkey.com) – This is a browser that is based on Internet Explorer, but specially designed to be user-friendly to younger children.

3. *CyberSitter* (http://www.pow-dist.co.uk) – This is a Windows95 program that lets you block access to common types of graphic files and other files and programs. You can set the software to block the files or to sound an alarm when your child tries to access them.

Rating systems

A rating system is based on an internationally agreed set of tools that can be used to control who sees what kind of content. Web sites rate themselves and include the rating information hidden on their web pages. Browsers can then access this information and decide whether the site is acceptable to the user or not. Sites with a rating that indicates that they are carrying unacceptable content are not shown. For the rating system to work, you must be using a browser capable of being configured for ratings. You will need to set these rating to the levels of tolerance you want it to exert.

In Microsoft's Internet Explorer, for example, you can find the rating system in Tools, Internet Options, Content and Content Advisor. Once you enable Content Advisor, a password is needed to bypass it.

PICS is now widely accepted as the main way to implement these ratings. It stands for Platform for Internet Content Selection. The most used set of standards for screening material was developed by the RSACi, the Recreational Software Advisory Council on the Internet. It rates material according to the degree of sex, violence, nudity, and bad language depicted. The levels and categories of the PICS/RSACi rating are shown in the table below.

Level	Violence	Nudity	Sex	Language
0	Harmless conflict, some damage to objects.	No nudity or revealing attire.	Romance, no sex.	Inoffensive slang, no profanity.
1	Creatures injured or killed, damage to objects, fighting.	Revealing attire.	Passionate kissing.	Mild expletives.
2	Humans injured, or small amounts of blood.	Partial nudity.	Clothed sexual touching.	Expletives, non-sexual anatomical references.
3	Humans injured or killed.	Non-sexual frontal nudity.	Non-explicit sexual activity.	Strong, vulgar language, obscene gestures, racial epithets.
4	Wanton and gratuitous violence, torture, rape.	Provocative frontal nudity.	Explicit sexual activity, sex crimes.	Crude or explicit sexual references, extreme hate speech.

The vast majority of sites on the web do not, and may never, use any ratings. Unless you allow your browser software to view unrated sites, your child will inevitably be blocked from many of the best sites on the web.

The problem of censoring internet content with a system like PICS is that there will always be conflicts of interest. Will pro-life activists want to ban abortion sites? Will pro-abortion supporters want to ban anti-abortion sites? What about animal cruelty and the question of fox hunting? The problem is not whether such sites should be filtered out. Rather, it is who will do the filtering. With PICS, the decision is largely taken out of your hands and, whatever the standards, you will lose out on great resources.

Besides, both Internet Explorer and Netscape are easy for any intelligent teenager to bypass. See page 77.

Exercising parental control
A third alternative is to rely on parental guidance and education. As with a television set, if a computer is in the child's bedroom, there is no foolproof way of ensuring that your child is not accessing something dubious or harmful. Always assume that your child knows more about the internet than you do. Unfortunately, the child may not have the common sense to avoid being harmed or conned by someone or by a web site on the internet.

Sharing the experience of the internet with your children will help you obtain the full benefits of the internet, and alert you to any potential problems that may await your child. If your children tell you about an upsetting incident, don't blame them. It is unlikely to be their fault. Help them to understand what has happened. How you respond to their problem will determine whether they confide in you the next time.

Never allow an internet-ready computer to remain in a child's bedroom. Besides possibly making the child less sociable, it can be an

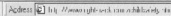

Address 🔲 http://www.right-track.com/childsafety.htm

Company Info
Home
Profile
Instructors
Clients
Testimonials
News
Contact

Training
Description
Courses
Class Schedule
Registration
Seminars

Other Services
Tech Support
Networks
App Development
Web Design
Classroom Rentals

RIGHT-TRACK

PERSONAL COMPUTER CENTER

Child Safety Links

Keeping children safe from harm is crucial to giving them the advantages of Internet access. Here are some links that explore the topic of child safety, including a few of the many "child-friendly" sites.

Information for Parents:

Child Safety on the Information Highway is probably the best and best-known writing on the subject. Written by Lawrence J. Magid, a syndicated columnist for the Los Angeles Times, this article separates the myths from the realities, explains what the risks are, includes guidelines for parents, and rules for children to abide by while on the Net.

Family PC's Kid Safety Clearinghouse, links regarding violence on the Net, Internet access at school and "kid-friendly" Net utilities.

Fig. 56. Like Cyberangels, Right-Track is a web site worth exploring. There are so many risks on the internet that it will pay you to take some defensive steps now.

open invitation for any stranger. Keep the computer in a shared room. Keep an eye on what is happening, or even better join in. If all else fails, you can lock it away when you leave the child alone in the house for any length or time.

Educate your children so that they know not to give out personal information such as name, address, phone number, email address, and name of school to anyone or any site on the internet without talking to you first.

You may have taught your child to avoid strangers in the street – but what is a stranger on the internet? Make sure that your child understands that a web site can collect information by using cartoon characters to act as representatives. Would your child trust his favourite cartoon character? How can you see a red fluffy bunny or a funny-faced clown as being harmful in any way?

If a total stranger stopped your child in the street and asked all kinds of personal questions about your family, you would be shocked. You might even report the incident to the police. But once your child goes on the internet the chance is that far more personal information will be asked for regularly and by many different 'strangers'.

A case study
In April 1999 *The Times* reported that a thirteen-year-old computer buff had run up a bill of £1.8 million on the internet. The boy had started out by trying to sell his friend as a slave on an online auctioneers called eBay. Although nobody bought his friend he was bitten by the auction bug and started to bid for goods himself. Three weeks later, the goods that he had bought included a 1955 sports car for $23,000, a Ford Convertible for

$24,500, and a bed from Canada allegedly worth $900,000. The boy admitted to journalists that he was in 'big trouble' with his mother.

It was first thought that he used his parents' password to gain access to eBay. However, it was later reported that he had his own account with eBay. The moral: always assume that your child's intelligence and skill will exceed his or her sense of responsibility. The only precaution that the parents could have taken in this case would have been to exercise some guidance, and better security with their passwords.

Protecting yourself against computer viruses

A computer virus can easily destroy days, months or years of work, yet still we often refuse to take sensible precautions. The mere mention of viruses puts fear into our hearts but not, it seems, into our minds. Even the most seasoned computer expert will occasionally ignore the advice that he throws around and loses work that he has not backed up.

If you insert disks into your computer, open email attachments, share disks, or download files from the internet, you could well encounter viruses. But one precaution everybody should take right now is to get some virus scanning software *now*. And once you have some, update it frequently new viruses appear every day.

Fig. 57. Dr Solomon's anti-virus software. Anti-virus software is import-ant, but you really need to use an up-to-date version. Good programs are regularly updated. Anything older than a month is useless. Update, now!

Antivirus software
Anti-virus software – virus scanners – may be almost as old as viruses but unfortunately no virus scanner is completely foolproof.

For practical reasons, anti-virus software is designed only to scan for the most common viruses. Therefore aim for software that promises regular and frequent updates. And get the latest updates. If you do this,

or better still if you use two scanners from different companies, you can be fairly certain that all known viruses will be detected.

An anti-virus software checklist
Good anti-virus software should:

1. Be up-to-date – you should obtain updates as soon as they are available.
2. Conform to standards set by the National Computer Security Association.
3. Be able to scan floppy disks, hard drives, CD-roms, and network drives.
4. Be able to monitor your computer while you are working, so it can warn you the second you try to open an infected file.
5. Include a version of the scanner that can be run on a bootable floppy disk.

Where do you get it?
Anti-virus software can be obtained from any computer retailer. Among the popular ones are McAfee, and Dr Solomon's AntivirusToolkit. One of the best is F-Prot, written by Fridrik Skulason in Iceland:

F-Prot
http://www.isvr.soton.ac.uk/ftp/pc/f-prot
'The English language shareware version of the program is available directly from Iceland,' says Fridrik. 'This version of the F-Prot anti-virus program is free of charge for private use (that is, free for any individual or family using it on a personally owned computer).' If you have internet access, you can download the latest version of F-Prot from here.

Download.Com
http://www.download.com
Here you can download other free anti-virus software such as Disinfectant for Macintosh and various trial versions of commercial anti-virus software.

Most anti-virus software scans your computer's memory seconds after you switch on. The software should display a warning if you try to open an infected file. Once an infected file is identified, most virus scanners will ask you if you want to clean the infected file or, if it cannot be cleaned, to delete it. Let the scanner clean or delete the infected file. Don't be tempted to ignore its existence or you will end up with many more infected files. Deleting is perhaps the safest option. (You have got backups of your own files, haven't you?)

As soon as you get an anti-virus program, make a copy of the bootable floppy, or create one and write-protect the disk (Start, Settings, Control Panel, Add/Remove Programs, Startup Disk). Keep the disk in a safe place away from dirt, children, pets and sources of magnetism such asTVs, speakers, and computer monitors.

If any anti-virus company claims that its program can detect any stealth virus, it is no more than a marketing trick. The only foolproof technique to detect stealth viruses is to cold-boot the computer: turn off the power, then on, with a clean write-protected bootable floppy, to ensure that no virus is present in memory. Then check the computer for viruses.

File attachments and file downloads
One of the main causes of virus infection is the file download. The precautions for downloading most files (except MicroSoft Office documents) are simple but must be strictly followed:

1. Don't open downloaded or attached files. Save them first.

2. Next, scan them with an up-to-date virus scanner before running or opening them. It may help to create a special 'quarantine' directory or folder on your hard drive for this purpose.

3. You may have changed your browser's settings so it can automatically open downloaded files. Disable this setting now. It may be cause you some inconvenience, but it could save you hours of work or even dismissal from your job.

4. Back up your files regularly and keep the backup disks in a safe place. Even though computer viruses are not airborne, this will help to keep the disks free from viruses. If a virus infects your system, clean the system then restore your files.

Some other actions that will make life a little less nerve-racking:

5. If you regularly receive documents as email attachments, ask for them to be sent as plain text files (*.txt) or Rich Text Format files (*.rtf), rather than as Word files (*.doc). This avoids the risk of macro viruses altogether.

6. Similarly, when you want to send a document to someone, send it as a plain text or rich text format file.

Oops, too late!
Sometimes a virus sneaks by all of your defences. It may have come from a game loaned to your children or from the illegal software that nobody will admit to having put there. Whatever the cause, it has happened. Stop everything, *now!*

1. Calm down. The virus has probably not destroyed your hard disk, but throwing the computer out of the window almost certainly will.

2. Get two cardboard boxes.

3. Use BIG writing and mark one box UNTESTED and the second as GOOD or TESTED. You will not need a third box labelled BAD. Use the bin for the infected disks that you can't clean.

4. Do a strict search of your house – toy cupboards, briefcases, secret

pockets. Get every floppy disk you can find.

5. Find the bootable floppy that came, or that you created, with your virus scanner.

6. If you have no virus scanner. Try to find and keep aside one bootable floppy that you are sure is clean. This is the crucial starting point, you must be certain that it is clean. Put the rest in the box marked UN-TESTED.

7. Do a clean reboot.

8. Turn off your computer, count to ten and, with the clean and write-protected, bootable floppy in the drive, start it up again. The computer will start from the floppy and thus stop the virus hiding itself.

9. Run your anti-virus software.

10. Find and, if possible, repair the infected files on your hard disk. If the damage is too great for the software to fix, delete the files and replace them with clean backups. Test the backups. You may also have to reinstall some software. Check the installation disks for viruses before you do.

11. Now check the floppy disks. One by one check each floppy. When clean, put the disk in the GOOD box. This way, if you are interrupted during your cleaning operation, you will at least know where to resume your purge. Destroy and bin any disks you can't clean.

12. Finally, to prevent a future disaster, install the virus scanner to work in the background so it guards your computer as you work. You might even consider keeping the computer locked away.

Virus Alerts
Anti-Virus Updates
Virus Library
▶ Virus Info Center
Recent Updates
Joke Programs
Trojans
Hoaxes
Web Viruses

Virus myths and hoaxes

Panic spreads easily, especially by email. All that is needed to start the flood is for one misinformed philanthropist to warn all of his friends and acquaintances about an email virus. The virus, they say, will erase the files on your hard drive or cause other damage if you read the email. Of course, those friends and acquaintances will also pass the message on. Thus the panic spreads. Of course, now that everyone is talking about it, there must be something in it. Is there?

The Computer Incident Advisory Capacity (CIAC) says of hoaxes: 'Since 1988, virus hoaxes have flooded the internet. With thousands of viruses worldwide, virus paranoia in the community has risen to an extremely high level. It is this paranoia that fuels virus hoaxes. A good example of this behaviour is the Good Times virus hoax which started in 1994 and is still circulating the internet today. Instead of spreading from one computer to another by itself, Good Times relies on people to pass it along.'

How do you identify a hoax? There are several signs:

1. If the warning sounds as if it is has been sent by an official organisation, or uses overly technical terms, it is probably a hoax because virus warnings are rarely sent to individuals unless it is part of a regular newsletter or mailing list.

2. Be especially alert if the warning urges you to pass it on to your friends. This should warn you straight away to be careful.

3. If the warning says that it is a Federal Communication Commission (FCC) warning, it is a hoax. The FCC have not sent, and never will send, warnings on viruses.

Always double-check before embarrassing yourself and clogging up the internet. Any of the usual news sites or mailing lists will pick up straight away on new viruses. The CIAC site above is especially useful in that it documents the hoaxes circulating around the internet as well as the genuine risks.

Another useful web site is the Computer Virus Myths home page:

Computer Virus Myths
http://www.kumite.com/myths
This contains descriptions of many known hoaxes.

More Internet Handbooks to help you

Protecting Children on the Internet
Shops & Shopping on the Internet
Using Credit Cards on the Internet
Your Privacy on the Internet

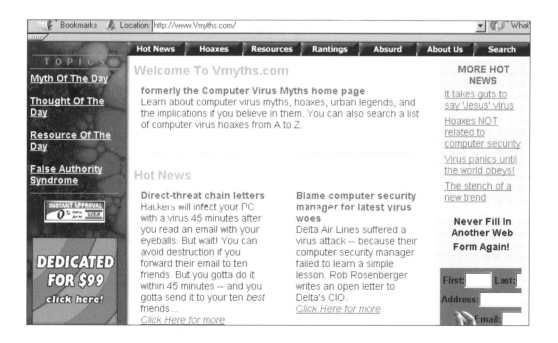

Appendix: Finding out more online

History of the internet

The History of the Internet
http://www.pbs.org/internet/timeline/

A Short History of the Internet by Bruce Sterling
http://info.isoc.org/guest/zakon/Internet/History/Short_History_of_the_Internet

Getting connected

Directory of Free ISPs
http://www.a2zweblinks.com/freeukisp/index.htm

Macintosh: Open Transport Help
http://www2.netdoor.com/-rreid/opentransport/

Windows: How to Set Up a Winsock Connection – A Beginner's Guide
http://omni.cc.purdue.edu/-xniu/winsock.htm

The world wide web

Newbie U's Web Stadium
http://www.newbie-u.com/web/

All About the World Wide Web
http://www.imaginarylandscape.com/helpweb/www/www.html

Sink or Swim: Internet Search Tools & Techniques
http://www.ouc.bc.ca/libr/connect96/search.htm

Search Engine Shoot-out: Search Engines Compared
http://www.cnet.com/Content/Reviews/Compare/Search2/

Email

Everything E-mail
http://everythingemail.net/

A Beginner's Guide to Effective Email
http://www.webfoot.com/advice/email.top.html

How to Find People's E-mail addresses
http://www.qucis.queensu.ca/FAQs/email/finding.html

Discussion forums

E-Mail Discussion Groups/Lists Resources
http://www.webcom.com/impulse/list.html

The List of Lists
http://catalog.com/vivian/interest-group-search.html

FTP: transferring files

Anonymous FTP – Frequently Asked Questions (FAQs)
http://www.cis.ohio-state.edu/hypertext/faq/usenet/ftp-list/faq/
faq.html

Multimedia File Formats on the Internet
http://www.lib.rochester.edu/multimed/intro.htm
Covers downloading files, file formats, ways to use the files, and ftp
software.

Privacy and security on the internet

Electronic Privacy Information Centre (EPIC)
http://www.epic.org
EPIC is a research centre in Washington. It was established in 1994 to
focus public attention on civil liberties issues and to protect privacy, the
First Amendment, and constitutional values. EPIC works in association
with the London human rights group Privacy International.

Internet Freedom
http://www.netfreedom.org
Internet Freedom is opposed to all forms of censorship and content regulation on the net, whether by government agencies or an increasing
number of pressure groups. The site mainly consists of news about the
many forms of censorship.

Privacy International
http://www.privacyinternational.org
Their site says, 'Privacy International is a human rights group formed in
1990 as a watchdog on surveillance by governments and corporations.
PI is based in London, and has an office in Washington, D.C. PI has conducted campaigns in Europe, Asia and North America to counter
abuses of privacy by way of information technology such as telephone
tapping, ID card systems, video surveillance, data matching, police
information systems, and medical records.'

Privacy Rights Clearing House
http://www.privacyrights.org
The PRC is a site that provides in-depth information on a variety of infor-
mational privacy issues, as well as giving tips on safeguarding your
personal privacy. The PRC was established with funding from the Telecommunications Education Trust, a program of the California Public
Utilities Commission.

Other Internet Handbooks to help you

Where to Find It on the Internet (Internet Handbooks, 2nd edition).

Visit the free Internet HelpZone at
www.internet-handbooks.co.uk
Helping you master the internet

87

Glossary of internet terms

access provider – The company that provides you with access to the internet. This may be an independent provider or a large international organisation such as AOL or CompuServe. See also **internet service provider**.

ActiveX – A programming language that allows effects such as animations, games and other interactive features to be included on a web page.

Adobe Acrobat – A type of software required for reading PDF files ('portable document format'). You may need to have Adobe Acrobat Reader when downloading large text files from the internet, such as lengthy reports or chapters from books. If your computer lacks it, the web page will prompt you, and usually offer you an immediate download of the free version.

address book – A directory in a web browser where you can store people's email addresses. This saves having to type them out each time you want to email someone. You just click on an address whenever you want it.

ADSL – (Asymmetric Digital Subscriber Line) is a modem technology that transforms ordinary phone lines into high-speed digital lines and can squeeze up to 99% more capacity out of them without interfering with your regular phone services. For example, you could talk on the phone and surf the world wide web at the same time.

AltaVista – One of the half dozen most popular internet search engines. Just type in a few key words to find what you want on the internet: http://www.altasvista.com

AOL – America OnLine, the world's biggest internet service provider, with more than 20 million subscribers, and now merged with Time Warner. Because it has masses of content of its own – quite aside from the wider internet – it is sometimes referred to as an 'online' service provider rather than internet service provider. It has given away vast numbers of free CDs with the popular computer magazines to build its customer base.

applet – An application programmed in Java that is designed to run only on a web browser. Applets cannot read or write data onto your computer, only from the domain in which they are served from. When a web page using an applet is accessed, the browser will download it and run it on your computer. See also **Java**.

application – Any program, such as a word processor or spreadsheet program, designed for use on your computer.

ARPANET – Advanced Research Projects Agency Network, an early form of the internet.

ASCII – American Standard Code for Information Interchange. It is a simple text file format that can be accessed by most word processors and text editors. It is a universal file type for passing textual information across the internet.

Ask Jeeves – A popular internet search engine. Rather than just typing in a few key words for your search, you can type in a whole question or instruction, such as 'Find me everything about online investment.' It draws on a database of millions of questions and answers, and works best with fairly general questions.

ASP – Active Server Pages, a filename extension for a type of web page.

attachment – A file sent with an email message. The attached file can be anything from a word-processed document to a database, spreadsheet, graphic, or even a sound or video file. For example you could email someone birthday greetings, and attach a sound track or video clip.

Authenticode – Authenticode is a system where ActiveX controls can be authenticated in some way, usually by a certificate.

avatar – A cartoon or image used to represent someone on screen while taking part in internet chat.

backup – A second copy of a file or a set of files. Backing up data is essential if there is any risk of data loss.

bandwidth – The width of the electronic highway that gives you access to the internet. The higher the bandwidth, the wider this highway, and the faster the traffic can flow.

banner ad – This is a band of text and graphics, usually situated at the top of a web page. It acts like a title, telling the user what the content of the page is about. It invites the visitor to click on it to visit that site. Banner advertising has become big business.

baud rate – The data transmission speed in a modem, measured in bps (bits per second).

BBS – Bulletin board service. A facility to read and to post public messages on a particular web site.

binary numbers – The numbering system used by computers. It only uses 1s and 0s to represent numbers. Decimal numbers are based on the number 10. You can count from nought to nine. When you count higher than nine, the nine is replaced with a 10. Binary numbers are based on the number 2: each place can only have the value of 1 or 0. You can count from nought to one. When you count higher than one, the one is replaced by 10 (not ten but one zero). Binary 10 would be equal to Decimal 2. For example:

Decimal	0	1	2	3	4	5	6	7	8	9	10
Binary	0	1	10	11	100	101	110	111	1000	1001	1010

Blue Ribbon Campaign – A widely supported campaign supporting free speech and opposing moves to censor the internet by all kinds of elected and unelected bodies.

Glossary ....

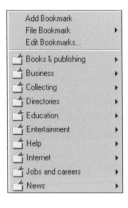

bookmark – A file of URLs of your favourite internet sites. Bookmarks are very easily created by bookmarking (mouse-clicking) any internet page you like the look of. If you are an avid user, you could soon end up with hundreds of them! In the Internet Explorer browser and AOL they are called 'favourites'.

boolean search – A search in which you type in words such as AND and OR to refine your search. Such words are called 'Boolean operators'. The concept is named after George Boole, a nineteenth-century English mathematician.

bot – Short for robot. It is used to refer to a program that will perform a task on the internet, such as carrying out a search.

browser – Your browser is your window to the internet, and will normally supplied by your internet service provider when you first sign up. It is the program that you use to access the world wide web, and manage your personal communications and privacy when online. By far the two most popular browsers are Netscape Communicator and its dominant rival Microsoft Internet Explorer. You can easily swap. Both can be downloaded free from their web sites and are found on the CD roms stuck to the computer magazines. It won't make much difference which one you use – they both do much the same thing. Opera, at http://www.opera.com is a great alternative that improves security, is faster and more efficient.

bug – A weakness in a program or a computer system.

bulletin board – A type of computer-based news service that provides an email service and a file archive.

cache – A file storage area on a computer. Your web browser will normally cache (copy to your hard drive) each web page you visit. When you revisit that page on the web, you may in fact be looking at the page originally cached on your computer. To be sure you are viewing the current page, press **reload** – or **refresh** – on your browser toolbar. You can empty your cache from time to time, and the computer will do so automatically whenever the cache is full. In Internet Explorer, pages are saved in the Windows folder, Temporary Internet Files. In Netscape they are saved in a folder called 'cache'.

certificate – A computer file that securely identifies a person or organisation on the internet.

CGI (common gateway interface) – This defines how the web server should pass information to the program, such as what it's being asked to do, what objects it should work with, any inputs, and so on. It is the same for all web servers.

channel (chat) – Place where you can chat with other internet chatters. The name of a chat channel is prefixed with a hash mark, #.

click through – This is when someone clicks on a banner ad or other link, for example, and is moved from that page to the advertiser's web site.

client – This is the term given to the program that you use to access the internet. For example your web browser is a web client, and your email program is an email client.

community – The internet is often described as a net community. This refers to the fact that many people like the feeling of belonging to a group of like-minded individuals. Many big web sites have been developed along these lines, such as GeoCities which is divided into special-interest 'neighbourhoods', or America OnLine which is strong on member services.

compression – Computer files can be electronically compressed, so that they can be uploaded or downloaded more quickly across the internet, saving time and money. If an image file is compressed too much, there may be a loss of quality. To read them, you uncompress 'unzip' them.

content – Articles, columns, sales messages, images, and the text of your web site.

content services – Web sites dedicated to a particular subject.

cookie – A cookie is a small code that the server asks your browser to keep until it asks for it. If it sends it with the first page and asks for it back before each other page, they can follow you around the site, even if you switch your computer off in between.

cracker – Someone who breaks into computer systems with the intention of causing some kind of damage or abusing the system in some way.

crash – What happens when a computer program malfunctions. The operating system of your PC may perform incorrectly or come to a complete stop ('freeze'), forcing you to shut down and restart.

cross-posting – Posting an identical message in several different newsgroups at the same time.

cybercash – This is a trademark, but is also often used as a broad term to describe the use of small payments made over the internet using a new form of electronic account that is loaded up with cash. You can send this money to the companies offering such cash facilities by cheque, or by credit card. Some internet companies offering travel-related items can accept electronic cash of this kind.

cyberspace – Popular term for the intangible 'place' where you go to surf – the ethereal and borderless world of computers and telecommunications on the internet.

cypherpunk – From the cypherpunk mailing list charter: 'Cypherpunks assume privacy is a good thing and wish there were more of it. Cypherpunks acknowledge that those who want privacy must create it for themselves and not expect governments, corporations, or other large, faceless organisations to grant them privacy out of beneficence. Cypherpunks know that people have been creating their own privacy for centuries with whispers, envelopes, closed doors, and couriers. Cypherpunks do not seek to prevent other people from speaking about their experiences or their opinions.'

Glossary ....

Dial-Up Networking

cypherpunk remailer – Cypherpunk remailers strip headers from the messages and add new ones.

data – Information. Data can exist in many forms such as numbers in a spreadsheet, text in a document, or as binary numbers stored in a computer's memory.

dial up account – This allows you to connect your computer to your internet provider's computer remotely.

digital – Based on the two binary digits, 1 and 0. The operation of all computers is based on this amazingly simple concept. All forms of information are capable of being digitalised – numbers, words, and even sounds and images – and then transmitted over the internet.

directory – On a PC, a folder containing your files.

DNS – Domain name server.

domain name – A name that identifies an IP address. It identifies to the computers on the rest of the internet where to access particular information. Each domain has a name. For someone@somewhere.-co.uk, 'somewhere' is the domain name. The domain name for Internet Handbooks for instance is: www.internet-handbooks.co.uk

download – 'Downloading' means copying a file from one computer on the internet to your own computer. You do this by clicking on a button that links you to the appropriate file. Downloading is an automatic process, except you have to click 'yes' to accept the download and give it a file name. You can download any type of file – text, graphics, sound, spreadsheet, computer programs, and so on.

ebusiness – The broad concept of doing business to business, and business to consumer sales, over the internet.

Echelon – The name of a massive government surveillance facility based in Yorkshire. Operated clandestinely by the US, UK and certain other governments, it is said to be eavesdropping virtually the entire traffic of the internet. It is said to use special electronic dictionaries to trawl through millions of emails and other transmissions.

ecommerce – The various means and techniques of transacting business online.

email – Electronic mail, any message or file you send from your computer to another computer using your 'email client' program (such as Netscape Messenger or Microsoft Outlook).

email address – The unique address given to you by your ISP. It can be used by others using the internet to send email messages to you. An example of a standard email address is:

mybusiness@aol.com

email bomb – An attack by email where you are sent hundreds or thousands of email messages in a very short period. This attack often prevents you receiving genuine email messages.

emoticons – Popular symbols used to express emotions in email. Emoticons are not normally appropriate for business communications. The best known is smiley :

:-) which means 'I'm smiling!'

encryption – The scrambling of information to make it unreadable without a key or password. Email and any other data can now be encrypted using PGP and other freely available programs. Modern encryption has become so powerful as to be to all intents and purposes uncrackable. Law enforcers worldwide want access to people's and organisation's passwords and security keys. In the UK you could be forced to hand over yours to the police, and face years in prison if you so much as talk about it (proposed Regulation of Investigatory Powers legislation, 2000).

Excite – A popular internet directory and search engine used to find pages relating to specific keywords which you enter. See also Yahoo!.

ezines – The term for magazines and newsletters published on the internet.

FAQ – Frequently asked questions. You will see 'FAQ' everywhere you go on the internet. If you are ever doubtful about anything check the FAQ page, if the site has one, and you should find the answers to your queries.

favorites – The rather coy term for **bookmarks** used by Internet Explorer, and by America Online. Maintaining a list of 'favorites' is designed to make returning to a site easier.

file – A file is any body of data such as a word-processed document, a spreadsheet, a database file, a graphics or video file, sound file, or computer program.

filtering software – Software loaded onto a computer to prevent access by someone to unwelcome content on the internet, notably porn. The well-known 'parental controls' include CyberSitter, Cyber-Patrol, SurfWatch and NetNanny. They can be blunt instruments. For example, if they are programmed to reject all web pages containing the word 'virgin', you would not be able to access any web page hosted at Richard Branson's Virgin Net! Of course, there are also web sites that tell you step-by-step how to disable or bypass these filtering tools.

finger – A tool for locating people on the internet. The most common use is to see if a person has an account at a particular internet site. It is also a chat command which returns information about the other chat user, including idle time (time since they last did anything).

firewall – A firewall is special security software designed to stop the flow of certain files into and out of a computer network, e.g. viruses or attacks by hackers. A firewall would be an important feature of any fully commercial web site.

flame – A more or less hostile or aggressive message posted in a news-group or to an individual newsgroup user. If they get out of hand there can be flame wars.

folder – The name for a directory on a computer. It is a place in which files (or other folders) are stored.

form – A web page that allows or requires you to enter information into fields on the page and send the information to a web site, program or individual on the web. Forms are often used for registration or sending questions and comments to web sites.

forums – Places for discussion on the internet. They include Usenet newsgroups, mailing lists, and bulletin board services.

frames – A web design feature in which web pages are divided into several areas or panels, each containing separate information. A typical set of frames in a page includes an index frame (with navigation links), a banner frame (for a heading), and a body frame (for text matter).

freebies – The 'give away' products, services or other enticements offered on a web site to attract registrations.

freespace – An allocation of free web space by an internet service provider or other organisation, to its users or subscribers.

freeware – Software programs made available without charge. Where a small charge is requested, the term is **shareware**.

front page – The first page of your web site that the visitor will see. FrontPage is also the name of a popular web authoring package from Microsoft.

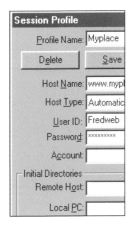

FTP – File transfer protocol: the method the internet uses to speed files back and forth between computers. Your browser will automatically select this method, for instance, when you want to download your bank statements to reconcile your accounts. In practice you don't need to worry about FTP unless you are thinking about creating and publishing your own web pages: then you would need some of the freely available FTP software. Despite the name, it's easy to use.

GIF – 'Graphic interchange format', a very common type of graphic file. It is a compressed file format used on web pages and elsewhere to display files that contain graphic images. See also JPEG.

GUI – Short for graphic user interface. It describes the user-friendly screens found in Windows and other WIMP environments (windows, icons, mouse, pointer).

hacker – A person interested in computer programming, operating systems, the internet and computer security. The term can be used to describe a person who breaks into computer systems with the intention of pointing out the weaknesses in a system. In common usage, the term is often wrongly used to describe crackers.

header – The header is that part of a message which contains information about the sender and the route that the message took through the internet.

history list – A record of visited web pages. Your browser probably includes a history list. It is handy way of revisiting sites whose addresses you have forgotten to bookmark – just click on the item you want in the history list. You can normally delete all or part of the history list in your browser. However, your ISP may well be keeping a record of your visits (see **internet service providers**, above).

hit counter – A piece of software used by a web site to publicly display the number of hits it has received.

hits – The number of times a web page has been viewed.

home page – This refers to the index page of an individual or an organisation on the internet. It usually contains links to related pages of information, and to other relevant sites.

host – A host is any computer where a particular file or domain is stored, and from where people can retrieve or access it.

HotBot – A popular internet search engine used to find pages relating to any keywords you decide to enter.

HTML – Hyper text markup language, the universal computer language used to create pages on the world wide web. It is much like word processing, but uses special 'tags' for formatting the text and creating hyperlinks to other web pages.

HTTP – Hypertext transfer protocol, the technical rules on which the world wide web is based. It is the language spoken between your browser and the web servers. It is the standard way that HTML documents are transferred from a host computer to your local browser when you're surfing the internet. You'll see the http acronym at the start of most web addresses, for example:

http://www.abcxyz.com

With modern browsers, it is no longer necessary to enter 'http://' at the start of the address. See also FTP.

hyperlink – See **link**.

hypertext – This is a link on an HTML page that, when clicked with a mouse, results in a further HTML page or graphic being loaded into view on your browser.

Infoseek – One of the ten most popular internet search engines.

internet – The broad term for the fast-expanding network of global computers that can access each other in seconds by phone and satellite links. If you are using a modem on your computer, you too are part of the internet. The general term 'internet' encompasses email, web pages, internet chat, newsgroups, and video conferencing. It is rather like the way we speak of 'the printed word' when we mean books, magazines, newspapers, newsletters, catalogues, leaflets, tickets and posters. The 'internet' does not exist in one place any more than 'the printed word' does.

Internet 2 – A new version of the internet being developed in the USA, intended for exclusive use by academic institutions and their members.

internet account – The account set up by your internet service provider which gives you access to the world wide web, electronic mail

- Top of Report
- General Statistics
- Most Requested Page
- Most Submitted Form
- Most Active Organizations
- Summary of Activity b Day
- Activity Level by Day Week
- Activity Level by Hou
- Technical Statistics

facilities, newsgroups and other services.

Internet Explorer – The world's most popular browser software, a product of Microsoft and leading the field against Netscape (now owned by America OnLine).

internet service providers – ISPs are commercial, educational or official organisations which offer people ('users') access to the internet. The well-known ones in the UK include AOL, CompuServe, BT Internet, Freeserve, Demon and Virgin Net. Commercial ISPs may levy a fixed monthly charge, though the world wide trend is now towards free services. Services typically include access to the world wide web, email and newsgroups, as well as news, chat, and entertainment. Your internet service provider may well know everything you do on the internet – emails you send and receive, the web sites you visit, information you downloaded, key words you type into search engines, newsgroups you visit and messages you read and post. In the UK, a new 'big brother' law forces your ISP to make all this information freely available to the police (Regulation of Investigatory Powers Act).

Internic – The body responsible for allocating and maintaining internet domain names: http://www.internic.net

intranet – A private computer network that uses internet technology to allow communication between individuals, for example within a large commercial organisation. It often operates on a LAN (local area network).

IP address – An 'internet protocol' address. All computers linked to the internet have one. The address is somewhat like a telephone number, and consists of four sets of numbers separated by dots.

IRC – Internet relay chat. Chat is an enormously popular part of the internet, and there are all kinds of chat rooms and chat software. The chat involves typing messages which are sent and read in real time. It was developed in 1988 by a Finn called Jarkko Oikarinen.

ISDN – Integrated Services Digital Network. This is a high-speed telephone network that can send computer data from the internet to your PC faster than a normal telephone line.

Java – A programming language developed by Sun Microsystems to use the special properties of the internet to create graphics and multimedia applications on web sites.

JavaScript – A simple programming language that can be put onto a web page to create interactive effects such as buttons that change appearance when you position the mouse over them.

jpeg – The acronym is short for Joint Photographic Experts Group. A JPEG is a specialised file format used to display graphic files on the internet. JPEG files are smaller than similar GIF files and so have become ever more popular – even though there is sometimes a feeling that their quality is not as good as GIF format files. See also MPEG.

key shortcut – Two keys pressed at the same time. Usually the 'control' key (Ctrl), 'Alt' key, or 'Shift' key combined with a letter or number. For example to use 'Control-D', press 'Control', tap the 'D' key once firmly then take your finger off the 'Control' key.

keywords – Words that sum up your web site for being indexed in search engines. For example for a cosmetic site the key words might include beauty, lipstick, make-up, fashion, cosmetic and so on.

kick – To eject someone from a chat channel.

LAN – A local area network, a computer network usually located in one building or campus.

link – A hypertext phrase or image that calls up another web page when you click on it. Most web sites have lots of hyperlinks, or 'links' for short. These appear on the screen as buttons, images or bits of text (often underlined) that you can click on with your mouse to jump to another site on the world wide web.

Linux – A freely available operating system for personal computers, and a potentially serious challenger to Microsoft Windows. Developed on DIY lines as open source software, it has developed a growing following.

listserver – An automated email system whereby subscribers are able to receive and send email from other subscribers to the list.

log on/log off – To access/leave a network. In the early days of computing this literally involved writing a record in a log book. You may be asked to 'log on' to certain sites and particular pages. This normally means entering your user ID in the form of a name and a password.

lurk – The slang term used to describe reading a newsgroup's messages without actually taking part in that newsgroup. Despite the connotations of the word, it is a perfectly respectable activity on the internet.

macros – 'Macro languages' are used to automate repetitive tasks in Word processors and other applications.

mail server – A remote computer through which you can send and receive emails. Your internet access provider will usually act as your mail server.

mailing list – A forum where messages are distributed by email to the members of the forum. The two types of lists are discussion and announcement. Discussion lists allow exchange between list members. Announcement lists are one-way only and used to distribute information such as news or humour. A good place to find mailing lists is Liszt (http://www.liszt.com). You can normally quit a mailing list by sending an email message to request removal.

marquee – A moving (scrolling) line of text, banner or other graphic on a web site, normally used for advertising purposes.

Glossary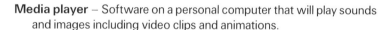

Media player – Software on a personal computer that will play sounds and images including video clips and animations.

metasearch engine – A site that sends a keyword search to many different search engines and directories so you can use many search engines from one place.

meta tags – The technical term for the keywords used in your web page code to help search engine software rank your site.

Mixmaster – An anonymous remailer that sends and receives email messages as packages of exactly the same size and often randomly varies the delay time between receiving and remailing to make interception harder.

modem – This is an internal or external piece of hardware plugged into your PC. It links into a standard phone socket, thereby connecting your computer to the internet. The word derives from MOdulator/DEModulator.

moderator – A person in charge of a mailing list, newsgroup or forum. The moderator prevents unwanted messages.

mpeg or **mpg** – The file format used for video clips available on the internet. See also JPEG.

MP3 – An immensely popular audio format that allows you to download and play music on your computer. It compresses music to create files that are small yet whose quality is almost as good as CD music. See http://mpeg.org for further technical information, or the consumer web site www.mp3.com. At time of writing, MP4, even faster to download, was being developed.

MUDs – Multi-User Dungeons, interactive chat-based fantasy world games. Popular in the early days of the internet, they are in now in decline with the advance of networked arcade games such as Quake and Doom.

navigate – To click on the hyperlinks on a web site in order to move to other web pages or internet sites.

net – A slang term for the internet. In the same way, the world wide web is often just called the web.

netiquette – Popular term for the unofficial rules and language people follow to keep electronic communication in an acceptably polite form.

Netmeeting – This Microsoft plug in allows a moving video picture to be contained within a web page. It is now integrated into Windows Media Player.

Netscape – After Microsoft's Internet Explorer, Netscape is the most popular browser software available for surfing the internet. An excellent browser, Netscape has suffered in the wake of Internet Explorer, mainly because of the success of Microsoft in getting the latter pre-loaded on most new PCs. Netscape Communicator comes complete with email, newsgroups, address book and bookmarks, plus a web page composer, and you can adjust its settings in all sorts of useful ways. Netscape was taken over by American Online for $4 billion.

nettie – Slang term for someone who likes to spend a lot of time on the internet.

newbie – Popular term for a new member of a newsgroup or mailing list.

newsgroup – A Usenet discussion group. Each newsgroup is a collection of messages, usually unedited and not checked by anyone ('unmoderated'). Messages can be placed within the newsgroup by anyone including you. It is rather like reading and sending public emails. The ever-growing newsgroups have been around for much longer than the world wide web, and are an endless source of information, gossip, news, entertainment, sex, politics, resources and ideas. The 80,000+ newsgroups are collectively referred to as Usenet, and millions of people use it every day.

news reader – A type of software that enables you to search, read, post and manage messages in a newsgroup. It will normally be supplied by your internet service provider when you first sign up, or preloaded on your new computer. The best known are Microsoft Outlook, and Netscape Messenger.

news server – A remote computer (e.g. your internet service provider) that enables you to access newsgroups. If you cannot get some or any newsgroups from your existing news server, use your favourite search engine to search for 'open news servers' – there are lots of them freely available. When you have found one you like, add it to your news reader by clicking on its name. The first time you do this, it may take 10 to 20 minutes to load the names of all the newsgroups onto your computer, but after that they open up in seconds whenever you want them.

nick – Nickname, – an alias you can give yourself and use when entering a chat channel, rather than using your real name.

Nominet – An official body for registering domain names in the UK (for example web sites whose name ends in .co.uk).

online – The time you spend linked via a modem to the internet. You can keep your phone bill down by reducing online time. The opposite term is offline.

open source software – A type of freely modifiable software, such as Linux. A definition and more information can be found at:
www.opensource.org

OS – The operating system in a computer, for example MS DOS (Microsoft Disk Operating System), or Windows 95/98/2000.

packet – The term for any small piece of data sent or received over the internet on your behalf by your internet service provider, and containing your address and the recipient's address. One email message for example may be transmitted as several different packets of information, reassembled at the other end to recreate the message.

password – A word or series of letters and numbers that enables a user to access a file, computer or program. A passphrase is a password made by using more than one word.

PC – Personal computer, not an Apple Macintosh.

PDA – Personal Data Assistant – a mobile phone, palm top or any other hand-held processor, typically used to access the internet.

Pentium – The name of a very popular microprocessor chip in personal computers, manufactured by Intel. The first Pentium IIIs were supplied with secret and unique personal identifiers, which ordinary people surfing the net were unwittingly sending out, enabling persons unknown to construct detailed user profiles. After a storm of protest, Pentium changed the technology so that this identifier could be disabled. If you buy or use a Pentium III computer you should be aware of this risk to your privacy when online.

PGP – Pretty Good Privacy. A proprietary method of encoding a message before transmitting it over the internet. With PGP, a message is first compressed then encoded with the help of keys. Just like the valuables in a locked safe, your message is safe unless a person has access to the right keys. Some governments (as in France today) demand complete access to people's private keys. New Labour also wants access to everyone's keys (including your bank's). Unlike many other countries, there is no general right to privacy in the UK.

ping – You can use a ping test to check the connection speed between your computer and another computer.

plug in – A type of (usually free and downloadable) software required to add some form of functionality to web page viewing. A well-known example is Macromedia Shockwave, a plug in which enables you to view animations.

PoP – Point of presence. This refers to the dial up phone numbers available from your ISP. If your ISP does not have a local point of presence (i.e. local access phone number), then don't sign up – your telephone bill will rocket because you will be charged national phone rates. All the major ISPs have local numbers covering the whole of the country.

portal site – Portal means gateway. It is a web site designed to be used as a starting point for your web experience each time you go online. Portals often serve as general information points and offer news, weather and other information that you can customise to your own needs. Yahoo! is an example of a portal (http://www.yahoo.com). A portal site includes the one that loads into your browser each time you connect to the internet. It could for example be the front page of your internet service provider. Or you can set your browser to make it some other front page, for example a search engine such as AltaVista, or even your own home page if you have one.

post, to – The common term used for sending ('posting') messages to a newsgroup. Posting messages is very like sending emails, except of course that they are public and everyone can read them. Also, newsgroup postings are archived, and can be read by anyone in the world years later. Because of this, many people feel more comfortable using an 'alias' (made-up name) when posting messages.

privacy – You have practically no personal privacy online. Almost every mouse click and key stroke you make while online is being electronically logged, analysed and possibly archived by internet organisations, government agencies, police and other surveillance services. You are also leaving a permanent trail of data on whichever computer you are using. But then, if you have nothing to hide you have nothing to fear from 'big brother'. To explore privacy issues worldwide visit the authoritative Electronic Frontier Foundation web site at www.eff.org, and for the UK, www.netfreedom.org

protocol – Technical term for the method by which computers communicate. A protocol is an agreed set of technical rules that can be used between systems. For example, for viewing web pages your computer would use hypertext transfer protocol (http). For downloading and uploading files, it would use file transfer protocol (ftp). It's not something to worry about in ordinary life.

proxy – An intermediate computer or server, used for reasons of security.

Quicktime – A popular free software program from Apple Computers. It is designed to play sounds and images including video clips and animations on both Apple Macs and personal computers.

radio button – A button which, when clicked, looks like this ⊙.

refresh, reload – The refresh or reload button on your browser toolbar tells the web page you are looking at to reload.

register – You may have to give your name, personal details and financial information to some sites before you can continue to use the pages. Site owners may want to produce a mailing list to offer you products and services. Registration is also used to discourage casual traffic which can clog up access.

registered user – Someone who has filled out an online form and then been granted permission to access a restricted area of a web site. Access is usually obtained by logging on, typically by entering a password and user name.

remailer – A remailer preserves your privacy by acting as a go between when you browse or send email messages. An anonymous remailer is simply a computer connected to the internet that can forward an email message to other people after stripping off the header of the messages. Once a message is routed through an anonymous remailer, the recipient of that message, or anyone intercepting it, can no longer identify its origin.

RSA – A popular method of encryption, and used in Netscape browsers. See http://www.rsa.com and see also PGP above.

router – A machine which directs – 'routes' – internet data (network packets) from one place to another.

Glossary ....

rules – The term for message filters in Outlook Express.

search engine – A search engine is a web site you can use for finding something on the internet. Popular search engines are big web sites and information directories in their own right. There are hundreds of them; the best known include Alta Vista, Excite, Google, Infoseek, Lycos and Yahoo!.

secure servers – The hardware and software provided so that people can use their credit cards and leave other details without the risk of others seeing them online. Your browser will tell you when you are entering a secure site.

secure sockets layer (SSL) – A standard piece of technology which encrypts and secures financial transactions and data flow over the internet.

security certificate – Information used by the SSL protocol to establish a secure connection. Security certificates contain information about who it belongs to, who it was issued by, some form of unique identification, valid dates, and an encrypted fingerprint that can be used to verify the contents of the certificate. In order for an SSL connection to be created both sides must have a valid security certificate.

server – Any computer on a network that provides access and serves information to other computers.

shareware – Software that you can try before you buy. Usually there is some kind of limitation such as an expiry date. To get the registered version, you must pay for the software, typically $20 to $40. A vast amount of shareware is now available on the internet.

Shockwave – A popular piece of software produced by Macromedia, which enables you to view animations and other special effects on web sites. You can download it free and in a few minutes from Macromedia's web site. The effects can be fun, but they slow down the speed at which the pages load into your browser window.

signature file – This is a little text file in which you can place your address details, for adding to email and newsgroup messages. Once you have created a signature file, it is appended automatically to your emails. You can of delete or edit it whenever you like.

Slashdot – One of the leading technology news web sites, found at: http://slashdot.org

smiley – A form of **emoticon**.

snail mail – The popular term for the standard postal service involving post-persons, vans, trains, planes, sacks and sorting offices.

spam – The popular term for electronic junk mail – unsolicited and unwelcome email messages sent across the internet. The term is borrowed from Monty Python. There are various forms of spam-busting software which you can now obtain to filter out unwanted email messages.

sniffer – A program on a computer system (usually an ISP's system) designed to collect information about internet use. Sniffers are often used by hackers to collect passwords and user names.

SSL – Secure socket layer, a key part of internet security technology.

subscribe – The term for accessing a newsgroup in order to read and post messages in the newsgroup. There is no charge, and you can subscribe, unsubscribe and resubscribe at will with a click of your mouse. Unless you post a message, no-one in the newsgroup will know that you have subscribed or unsubscribed.

surfing – Slang term for browsing the internet, especially following trails of links on pages across the world wide web.

sysop – Systems operator, someone rather like a moderator for example of a chat room or bulletin board service.

TCP/IP – Transmission control protocol/internet protocol, the essential technology of the internet. It's not normally something to worry about.

telnet – Software that allows you to connect via the internet to a remote computer and work as if you were at a terminal linked to that system.

theme – A term in web page design. A theme describes the general colours and graphics used within a web site. Many themes are available in the form of readymade templates.

thumbnail – A small version of a graphic file.

thread – An ongoing topic in a Usenet newsgroup or mailing list discussion. The term refers to the original message on a particular topic, and all the replies and other messages which spin off from it. With news reading software, you can easily 'view thread' and thus read the related messages in one convenient batch.

traceroute – A program that traces the route of a communication between your machine and a remote system. It is useful if you need to discover a person's ISP, for example in the case of a spammer.

traffic – The amount of data flowing across the internet to a particular web site, newsgroup or chat room, or as emails.

trojan horse – A program that seems to perform a useful task but is really a malevolent one designed to cause damage to a computer system.

uploading – The act of copying files from your PC to a server or other PC on the internet, for example when you are publishing your own web pages. The term is most commonly used to describe the act of copying HTML pages onto the internet via FTP.

UNIX – This is a computer operating system that has been in use for many years, and still is used in many larger systems. Most ISPs use it.

URL – Uniform resource locator the address of each internet page. For instance the URL of Internet Handbooks is http://www.internet-handbooks.co.uk

Glossary ....

Usenet – The collection of well over 80,000 active newsgroups that make up a substantial part of the internet.

virtual reality – The presentation of a lifelike scenario in electronic form. It can be used for gaming, business or educational purposes.

virus – A computer program maliciously designed to cause havoc to people's computer files. Viruses can typically be received when downloading program files from the internet, or from copying material from infected disks. Even Word files can now be infected. You can protect yourself from the vast majority of them by installing some inexpensive anti-virus software, such as Norton, McAfee or Dr Solomon.

WAP – Wireless Application Protocol, new technology that enables mobile phones to access the internet.

web authoring – Creating HTML pages to upload onto the internet. You will be a web author if you create your own home page for uploading onto the internet.

web client – Another term for a browser such as Internet Explorer or Netscape Navigator.

Webcrawler – A popular internet search engine used to find pages relating to specific keywords entered.

webmaster – Any person who manages a web site.

web page – Any single page of information you can view on the world wide web. A typical web page includes a unique URL (address), headings, text, images, and hyperlinks (usually in the form of graphic icons, or underlined text). One web page usually contains links to lots of other web pages, either within the same web site or elsewhere on the world wide web.

web rings – A network of interlinked web sites that share a common interest.

whois – A network service that allows you to consult a database containing information about someone. A whois query can, for example, help to find the identity of someone who is sending you unwanted email messages.

Windows – The ubiquitous operating system for personal computers developed by Bill Gates and the Microsoft Corporation. The Windows 3.1 version was followed by Windows 95, further enhanced by Windows 98. Windows 2000 is the latest.

WWW – The world wide web. Since it began in 1994 this has become the most popular part of the internet. The web is now made up of more than a billion web pages of every imaginable description, typically linking to other pages. Developed by the British computer scientist, Tim Berners-Lee, its growth has been exponential and is set to continue so.

WYSIWYG – 'What you see is what you get.' If you see it on the screen, then it should look just the same when you print it out.

Yahoo! – Probably the world's most popular internet directory and search engine, and now valued on Wall Street at billions of dollars: http://www.yahoo.com

zip/unzip – Many files that you download from the internet will be in compressed format, especially if they are large files. This is to make them quicker to download. These files are said to be zipped or compressed. Unzipping these compressed files means returning them to their original size. Zip files have the extension '.zip' and are created (and unzipped) using WinZip or a similar compression software package.

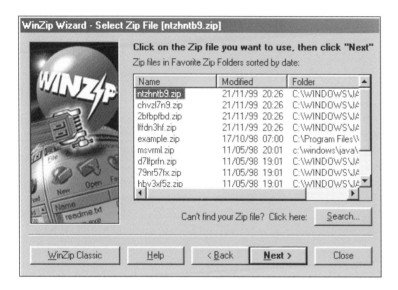

Index

Index ....

Creating a Home Page on the Internet
An illustrated step-by-step guide for beginners
Richard Cochrane BA(Hons) PhD

Have you just started to use the internet? Or perhaps you are still wondering whether to take the plunge? Either way, you will soon be wondering how you can produce and publish web pages of your own, as millions of other individuals have done all over the world. It's easy! Discover how to design a simple but effective home page; see how to add your own artwork and photographs; learn how to add those magic hypertext links that enable you to click effortlessly from one web page to another. Finally, explore how you can actually publish your own home pages in cyberspace, where potentially anyone in the world can pay you a 'visit' and contact you by email.
1 84025 309 6

Finding a Job on the Internet
Amazing new possibilities for jobseekers everywhere
Brendan Murphy BSc (Hons)

Thinking of looking for a new job, or even a change of career? The internet is a really great place to start your job search. In easy steps and plain English, this new Internet handbook explains how to find and use internet web sites and newsgroups to give you what you need. School, college and university leavers will find it a valuable resource for identifying suitable employers and getting expert help with CVs and job applications. The book will also be useful for employers thinking of using the internet for recruitment purposes, and for career and training advisers everywhere.
1 84025 310 X – reprinted

Gardens & Gardening on the Internet
A practical handbook and reference guide to horticulture online
Judith & Graham Lawlor MA

Gardeners are often in need of specific information to help them in their projects, and the internet is proving an amazingly valuable new aid to modern gardening. This new book leads you quickly and painlessly to some amazing new gardening help lines, retail and wholesale suppliers, online clubs and societies, and web sites devoted to such topics as rare plants, water gardens, celebrity gardening, gardening holidays, and horticultural science. The book will be absolutely indispensable for all gardeners with access to the internet.
1 84025 313 4

Other Internet Handbooks ....

Homes & Property on the Internet
A guide to 1000s of top web sites for buyers, sellers, owners, tenants, sharers, holidaymakers & property professionals
Philip Harrison

Here is a guide to today's whole new world of homes and property services online. Here are web sites of every imaginable kind for estate agents, house builders, removal firms, decorators, town planners, architects and surveyors, banks and building societies, home shares, villa owners and renters, and property-related associations, pressure groups, newspapers and magazines. Whether you are planning to move house, or rent a holiday home, or locate property services in the UK or wider afield, this is the book for you – comprehensive and well-indexed to help you find what you want.
1 84025 335 5

Medicine & Health on the Internet
A practical guide to online advice, treatments, doctors and support groups
Sarah Wilkinson

In the last couple of years, thousands of new health and medical web sites have been launched on the internet. Do you want to find out about a specialist treatment or therapy? Do you want to contact a support group or clinician online, or perhaps just get the answer to a simple question? Don't get lost using search engines. Whether you are a patient, relative, carer, doctor, health administrator, medical student or nurse, this book will lead you quickly to all the medical and health resources you need – help lines, support groups, hospitals, clinics and hospices, health insurance and pharmaceutical companies, treatments, suppliers, professional bodies, journals, and more.
1 84025 337 1

Personal Finance on the Internet
Your complete online guide to savings, investment, loans, mortgages, pensions, insurance and all aspects of personal finance
Graham Jones BSc (Hons)

For many people the internet is now the preferred means of managing their personal finances. But how do you do it? Where can you check out financial products and services on the internet? How secure is it, and what are the risks? Step-by-step this book describes the emerging world of online personal finance. It explains what you need to run your finances on the internet, where to find financial information, managing your bank account online, getting credit via the internet, checking out mortgages online, saving your money online, buying and selling stocks and shares online, arranging your pensions and insurance online, paying taxes, and much more.
1 84025 320 7

Protecting Children on the Internet
An effective approach for parents and teachers
Graham Jones BSc (Hons)

Are you concerned that children in your care might view unsuitable material on the internet? Without the right protection, children can easily stumble across pornography, violence, sexism, racism, and other damaging material. This book tells you step-by-step how to make sure that your youngsters are free to get the best from the internet, whilst shielding them from the worst. Using practical examples, it explains how to set up your web browser to protect them, how to use parental controls and filtering software to exclude unwelcome content from your child's screen, and so ensure a positive experience of this powerful new medium.
1 84025 344 4

Shops & Shopping on the Internet
A practical guide to online stores, catalogues, retailers and shopping malls
Kathy Lambert

In the last couple of years, thousands of shops and stores have been launched on the internet. But what are they like? Where can you find your favourite brands and stores? What about deliveries from suppliers in the UK or overseas? Can you safely pay by credit card? Don't get stuck in the internet traffic! This carefully structured book will take you quickly to all the specialist stores, virtual shopping malls, and online catalogues of your choice. You will be able to compare prices, and shop till you drop for books, magazines, music, videos, clothes, holidays, electrical goods, games and toys, wines, and a vast array of other goods and services.
1 84025 327 4

Travel & Holidays on the Internet
The amazing new world of online travel services, information, prices, reservations, timetables, bookings and more
Graham Jones BSc (Hons)

Thinking of checking out flights to Europe or America, or booking a package holiday? The internet is the best place to start. In easy steps and plain English, this book explains how to find and use the web to locate the travel and holiday information you need. You can view the insides of hotels, villas and even aeroplanes, quickly compare costs and services, and make your reservations and bookings securely online. All the big holiday and travel companies are now online – from airlines to the major tour operators but you'll be amazed at how much more you'll find with the help of this remarkable book.
1 84025 325 8

Using Credit Cards on the Internet
A practical step-by-step guide for all cardholders and retailers
Graham Jones BSc (Hons)

Are you worried about using credit cards on the internet? Do you know the truth about 'secure transactions'? Would you like to know how to get a special online credit card? This valuable new book shows you how to avoid trouble and use your 'virtual plastic' in complete safety over the internet. It contains all the low-down on security, practical tips to make sure that all your credit card dealings are secure, and advice on where to find credit cards with extra 'web protection'. It also show how to apply online for a new credit card, and how to use certain other forms of payments now widely accepted over the internet. If you are running a business on the internet, it also explains how to set up a 'merchant account' so that customers can safely pay you using their credit cards. The book is complete with a guide to the best sites on credit card usage.
1 84025 349 5

Using Email on the Internet
A step-by-step guide to sending and receiving messages and files
Kye Valongo

Email is one of the oldest parts of the internet. Most newcomers approach it with a bit of trepidation. But don't worry – it is quite straightforward and easy. By the time you have finished reading this book you will be happily sending emails across the world and not even flinching. Emailing is fast, cheap and convenient, and you'll soon wonder how you ever managed without it. Use this book to find out how to get started, how to successfully send and receive your first messages, how to send and receive attached files, how to manage your email folders, address book, user profiles, personal privacy, and lots more valuable skills.
1 84025 300 2

Where to Find It on the Internet (2nd edition)
Your complete guide to search engines, portals, databases, yellow pages & other internet reference tools
Kye Valongo

Here is a valuable basic reference guide to hundreds of carefully selected web sites for everyone wanting to track down information on the internet. Don't waste time with fruitless searches – get to the sites you want, fast. This book provides a complete selection of the best search engines, online databases, directories, libraries, people finders, yellow pages, portals, and other powerful research tools. A recent selection of 'The Good Book Guide', and now in a new edition, this book will be an essential companion for all internet users, whether at home, in education, or in the workplace.
1 84025 369 X – 2nd edition